SIGNALS

of

TRANSCENDENCE

Listening *to the* Promptings *of* Life

OS GUINNESS

An imprint of InterVarsity Press
Downers Grove, Illinois

InterVarsity Press
P.O. Box 1400 | Downers Grove, IL 60515-1426
ivpress.com | email@ivpress.com

InterVarsity Press® is the publishing division of InterVarsity Christian Fellowship/USA®. For more information, visit intervarsity.org.

All Scripture quotations, unless otherwise indicated, are taken from the New American Standard Bible®, copyright 1960, 1962, 1963, 1968, 1971, 1972, 1973, 1975, 1977, 1995 by The Lockman Foundation. Used by permission.

While any stories in this book are true, some names and identifying information may have been changed to protect the privacy of individuals.

Published in association with the literary agency of Wolgemuth & Associates.

Portions of the introduction and chapter three are adapted from *Fool's Talk* by Os Guinness. Copyright © 2015 by Os Guinness. Used by permission of InterVarsity Press, Downers Grove, IL.

The publisher cannot verify the accuracy or functionality of website URLs used in this book beyond the date of publication.

Cover design and image composite: David Fassett
Interior design: Jeanna Wiggins

ISBN 978-1-5140-0439-5 (print) | ISBN 978-1-5140-0440-1 (digital)

Printed in the United States of America ♾

Library of Congress Cataloging-in-Publication Data
Names: Guinness, Os, author.
Title: Signals of transcendence : listening to the promptings of life / Os Guinness.
Description: Downers Grove, IL : IVP, [2023]	Includes index.
Identifiers: LCCN 2022046019 (print)	LCCN 2022046020 (ebook)	ISBN 9781514004395 (print)	ISBN 9781514004401 (digital)
Subjects: LCSH: Transcendence (Philosophy)	Transcendence of God.
Classification: LCC BD362 .G84 2023 (print)	LCC BD362 (ebook)	DDC 141/.3–dc23/eng/20230120
LC record available at https://lccn.loc.gov/2022046019
LC ebook record available at https://lccn.loc.gov/2022046020

29 28 27 26 25 24 23 | 13 12 11 10 9 8 7 6 5 4 3 2

DOM

And in memory of Peter L. Berger,

whose own comic genius and profound insights

were the catalyst for this book.

CONTENTS

ACKNOWLEDGMENTS

T his book owes its genesis to my friend and mentor Peter L. Berger, and in particular to his little book *A Rumor of Angels*. I also owe a great debt to Kevin and Bonnie McKernan for many happy hours of conversation as well as their close reading of the first draft of this book. Their criticisms were as sure as their suggestions were invaluable.

INTRODUCTION

I 'm at a point in my life where I realize that there has to be more to life. Something must be missing."

This remark, made to me by a business leader in Silicon Valley, expresses what countless people come to see in their own way and say in their own words. Previously, they were mostly contented in some season of life; some were wealthy, successful, and even highly celebrated in one field or another. But they reached a point where they knew in their heart of hearts that none of it quite satisfied as they hoped. Who am I? Why am I here? What is life all about?

Life raises such questions to all of us at some point, and certain experiences break into our lives that spur us to question whether our answers are deep enough, prompting a search for what we sense is missing—an unnamable *something more*. Life itself is extraordinary, and somehow we all want to know what it is to live a worthy life, one that fulfills the promise of life.

Peter Berger, the eminent social scientist, described the experiences that trigger such longings as "signals of transcendence"— arresting and intriguing experiences that both capture our attention and call for further explanation. The thrust of these signals points to some meaning beyond themselves, and they won't let us off the hook until we stir ourselves to find what it is. Such experiences puncture one's satisfaction with the status quo and push one to search for something beyond.

The signals stir in us a sense that there must be something more to life, but what is that often unnamable something? In stirring us, signals of transcendence are a prompting by life itself, as it were. They trigger both a contradiction and a desire, and call into question the past, the present, and the future. They challenge the present and the past by contradicting the temptation to settle down and be satisfied. They challenge the future by spurring a desire to search for the *something* that is missing, that toward which the experience is hinting.

In so doing, the signals lay bare some aspect of our human existence that we have forgotten or suppressed, at least partially—including things lost and left behind. Such aspects of a fuller and more complete reality must be rediscovered if life is to be lived to the full. Equally, an understanding of those aspects has to be grounded solidly if it is to be truly fulfilling. Hence the quest for faith and meaning triggered by the signals—the quest for meaning that is adequate and faith that is true. Follow the signals and discover more of the reality of who we are and what the universe and life are about; then our lives will be better aligned and more able to be free and fulfilled. Freedom, after all, is simply the ability to be who we are, to think freely, to speak freely, and to act freely. But who in truth are we, why are we here, and what is life about? The signal is power packed with the thrust of such questions.

People have used a myriad of words to describe such signals of transcendence. They have been called "clues," "hints," "spurs," "jolts," "triggers," "homing signals," "points of bafflement," "scene shifters," "epiphanies," "mini paradigm shifts," "holes torn in the wall," and "metaphysical hunger pangs." But they all describe experiences that make people realize there must be something more in life than they had imagined, experiences that beckon them to the door of what poet William Wordsworth called "worlds not realized."

The Irish have a term, *thin places*, which they use to describe places or experiences where the membrane between the seen and the unseen, the natural and the supernatural, is barely there and easily penetrated. Heaven and earth are only a few feet apart, the Celts say, but in thin places they are even closer. Experiencing a signal of transcendence is like having a knife thrust through the membrane in thin places.

Berger set out a fascinating series of examples of such signals of transcendence in one chapter of his little classic, *A Rumor of Angels*. Originally, he had put more weight on the signals, expecting them to be signals that also went on to deliver the substance of what they pointed to. But he came to see that the experiences were no more than signals, signposts in sound. People who hear the signals have to follow where they lead and look for the answers themselves. The signals only signal. They themselves do not deliver the satisfaction of the discoveries, and any "leap of faith" from the signals to the hoped-for satisfaction would be wrong. Faith requires a warranted step—not a leap in the dark. Yet by their very thrust, the signals rule out some answers and suggest others, and they launch a search. True searchers are those who then follow the signals and set out on the journey. Follow the truth where it leads, the signals say. There is more to you, and there is more to life for you to discover for your own good.

Peter Berger's idea of the signals of transcendence has resonated deeply with many people. He was my mentor and friend, and we discussed writing a book together that expanded on his original thoughts. Sadly, his death made that partnership impossible, but this little book is my own offering of the same idea—in the form of stories.

SHADOWS OR SUNSHINE?

The core idea behind the stories in this book is simple. Such is the human condition that the promptings of life and the longing for something more are nearly universal, and are far more common than often admitted or usually understood. Such signals of transcendence can be heard, beeping insistently throughout life for those who listen. Curiously, the experiences of these signals have a decidedly subversive character in today's world. The advanced modern world has a lopsided view of reality and of how truth may be found. It majors on what can be known through rational logic and sensory perception, so that scientific observation and experimentation form the main body of modern knowledge. The effect is to minimize intuition, even though intuition plays an undeniable part in all creativity and discovery, whether artistic or scientific. Archimedes' "Eureka!" and Isaac Newton's response to the falling apple were a matter of intuition and not observation; so too were the creative breakthroughs of Galileo, William Shakespeare, Johann Sebastian Bach, Wolfgang Amadeus Mozart, Ludwig van Beethoven, and countless others.

Overall, this shrunken view of truth and modern knowledge acts to form a gigantic global conspiracy against transcendence. It has become a prominent but unfortunate feature of modern civilization, which helps us to be superachievers materially but underachievers spiritually. It patrols the boundaries of what modernity considers real and unreal. As modern people, we have grown unused to the sound of any voice beyond the immediate and the urgent. Signals of transcendence require a listening that is attention at its best. But while the signals are harder to hear today, they are more important than ever to hear. The *how* and the *what* of life rush at us every day with their urgency, but the *why* is even more important, and that is where we must begin if we desire to explore the whole of reality and discover true meaning and purpose.

Plato captured the importance of knowing what is real and unreal in his famous parable of the cave, as told by Socrates in *The Republic*. A group of prisoners has been given a life sentence and is chained in a cave. All they can see are flickering shadows cast on the blank wall in front of them, as people and objects move between them and a fire that is behind them at the back of the cave. The shadows on the wall are the only reality the prisoners can see, and they have developed their own full set of terms to understand and describe them.

The wise man, Socrates argues, is like a prisoner who has escaped from the cave. In the bright light of the sun, he realizes that the flickering shadows on the wall are not the complete reality at all. They are appallingly inadequate compared with reality. He returns to tell the good news to his fellow inmates, but they are incredulous. What he is saying is incomprehensible and disturbing to those still inside the cave. The shadows are the only reality they know, so to them the sunlight is unreal, and they are reluctant to leave the only world they know in case the search turns out to be a fool's errand. Such as it is, shadows and all, life in the cave is reality enough for them. It's nothing to sing about or celebrate, but it is the only life they know, and they have grown used to it. So, they choose to stay where they are rather than run the risk of disappointment in attempting to get outside and finding there is nothing there.

A WORLD WITHOUT WONDER

The cave dwellers, for Plato, were a picture of the human condition. And in many ways, they are even more apt as a picture of our condition in the advanced modern world—for several reasons. First, growing up in any generation is a process of asking fewer and fewer questions and experiencing less and less wonder. When we were children, questions, wonder, and curiosity were as natural as breathing, and our flow of questions often had to be cut off by our parents. They were too busy as adults to respond to the endless insistence of our "Why this? Why that?" But now that we are adults ourselves, the unrelenting speed, stuff, stress, and seriousness of life squeeze out all wonder and curiosity from our lives, especially if we live our days in ever-expanding cityscapes where everything is humanly designed, humanly constructed, and artificial from beginning to end. Hyperreality and the much-discussed "metaverse" will only compound this handicap.

Like our parents before us, we in our turn soon find ourselves pressed for time in the 24/7 world of supermodern fast-life. Pausing to question anything in a profound way is a luxury we can no longer afford. Atheists have sometimes mocked faith for being infantile, a child's view of reality, but the truth boomerangs. Children are as instinctively questioning as they are naturally religious and full of wonder about life. The combination is telling, and it says as much about adults as about children.

As life goes on, the problem is compounded further. Scholarship goes about its explaining, journalism its reporting, management its controlling, punditry its predicting, and modern education its instructing, and there is less and less room to question anything or have any sense of wonder. In the form of multiple-choice tests, there is an assumption that the best assessment of wisdom is the right answer, and the right answer is always the answer that is known ahead. The same is true of the trial lawyer, trained only to ask questions of which he is sure of the answers. But the fallacy is obvious. The right answer may be an accurate assessment of knowledge in the form of information already mastered, but the true test of wisdom and the best way to lead a life of creative thinking is the ability to ask the right questions, to keep on asking questions, and always to be prepared to go beyond what we know now, in order to discover something new.

A WORLD WITHOUT WINDOWS

Second, as citizens of the advanced modern world, we live in what Berger calls "a world without windows," the materialistic shadow world of Plato's cave with official scorn for any mention of the sun or a world outside. Our official, paramount, and dominant "reality" is the seven-to-eleven daytime world, which is shaped and limited by the reach of our five senses—reality is what we can see, hear, touch, smell, and taste—and therefore measure and calculate. This is the world we hail today as the "real world," and as Berger says, its reality is dense, heavy, and compelling. From time to time we slip the leash of this real world, above all when we sleep and dream. But we can also exit it in other ways, such as through a joke, a book, a film, or drink and drugs, and of course through quantum mechanics. But waking up, putting the book down, stepping out of the cinema, or simply sobering up, we know we are back in the cast-iron solidity of the real world, which is all there is, all there was, and all there ever will be.

For our ancestors, and for most humans in history, the world was larger than the material world of the five senses. The daytime, waking world was only the *seen* world, and the seen world was not the only world. In fact, for most people in history the unseen world—however it was understood—was as real, if not more real, than the seen world. Things in the seen world that were as practical and down to earth as making business decisions or making love were understood in light of the unseen world.

For most people today, however, the seen world is all there is. The seen is real and the unseen is unreal. There is nothing else. Without realizing it, we live in a windowless world, and in Max Weber's words, we are unmusical and tone-deaf to anything else. We are unable and unconcerned to listen to what Albert Einstein called the music of the spheres, or to entertain any thought that might come from outside our little lives and their well-insulated cocoons. Our view of reality, as G. K. Chesterton put it, is no better than that of a slightly drowsy middle-aged man right after a good lunch.

To change the picture to another famous parable from Greece, we modern people are like the guests of the Greek innkeeper Procrustes. We have been forced to fit onto a bed that is too small for us. As philosopher Abraham Heschel expressed, "The agony of the contemporary man is the agony of a spiritually stunted man. The image of man is larger than the frame into which he has been compressed." As modern people, we are schooled to believe that science, technology, the democratic state, and the free-market economy will supply all our needs and answer all our questions. And to be sure, we live with the privilege of options most generations could only dream of. Yet the superabundant how and what of modern life will never drown out the why—though try engaging your friends and colleagues with an understanding that goes beyond the material, the measurable, and the rationally reckonable, and you are sure to be eyed askance.

WEAPONS OF MASS DISTRACTION

Third, there are practical reasons why it makes good sense to avoid thinking more widely and deeply, at least in the short run. We humans have always resorted to what French mathematician Blaise Pascal called "diversions," and our advanced modern world provides the grandest diversions ever designed. Those whose lives are spent in triple-screen gazing (the mobile phone, the computer, and the television) can barely see beyond the end of their noses—and are all the happier for it. In T. S. Eliot's words, we humans cannot bear too much reality, and the ultimate reality is that we all may suffer and we all will die. Many of us have not included death, our own or others, into the equations that make up our sense of the meaning of life. So, it makes a certain shortsighted sense to surround ourselves with busy, entertaining distractions. If we succeed in diverting ourselves royally, we won't have to think or care too deeply about anything unpleasant. But the outcome has been to stifle our questioning and our wonder even more. With our modern lack of time and our endless supply of modern technological devices and gadgets, such diversions become "weapons of mass distraction" so that we never have to think deeply at all.

The net effect of all these factors is that many modern people live all their lives as if in Plato's cave, unaware and unconcerned. They have no idea and are probably skeptical that there is any other reality than the seven-to-eleven world in which we live every day. They have lost their sense of questioning, wonder, and curiosity, and they live under a powerful spell that the seen world is all there is. The insistent ordinariness of our daily existence drowns out the wonder of existence itself, and we don't notice the huge gap between the two levels of reality.

THE ANIMAL THAT ASKS AND ASKS

Properly understood, wonder, curiosity, and questioning are invaluable keys to life. They trigger the search for the meaning of life. They fire and fuel grand enterprises, such as scientific discovery and journalistic investigation. They motivate desire for pursuing the good life, and they form a vital part of the secret of finishing well. After all, as the literary critic George Steiner claims, we humans are not so much *Homo sapiens* as *Homo quaerens*, "the animal that asks and asks." Or as philosopher-rabbi Jonathan Sacks puts it, "We are the one life form known to us that can ask the question, 'Why?'"

Wonder and curiosity begin in the face of the cosmos itself. Philosophy too. "Why is there not nothing?" Or "Why is there something rather than nothing?" Gottfried Leibniz, the famous seventeenth-century philosopher and mathematician, raised that question as he pondered the wonder of our highly improbable universe. Vast, mysterious, and wonderful in itself—and all the more so as we probe and discover it further today—the universe is nowhere more awesome than in the sheer fact that it exists at all. But why does it exist? Who or what brought existence into being? What sort of odds would there have to be for such beauty, wonder, harmony, and complexity to be purely the product of chance?

Life on earth is wonderful too. Thrusting, teeming, colorful, and diverse in all its forms, life is filled with many-splendored wonders that are impossible to miss when we think of all it took for them all to have happened in the way they have. A few differences here and a few differences there, and it would all be so different. In fact, only a very few fine-tuned differences more and our universe could simply never have been. Why then is it as it is?

Our own humanity is out of the ordinary as well, and the great classics of the world present a resounding chorus of witness to the marvel and the paradox of human beings. As I wrote in an earlier book, we humans are so small yet so great, so strong and so weak. We rise so high and we sink so low. We are body and we are spirit. We are mortal and we are immortal. We have grandeur and we have pathos. We create and we kill. We build Gothic cathedrals and we build death camps. Sometimes our little lives seem like a momentary fleck on the heaving swell of the ocean, yet we are the center of our own universe while we live, and together as humanity we are the most powerful and influential creatures on our tiny, blue ball of a planet. Are we God's masterpiece? Accidental freak misfits and a cosmic error? Or what?

Why is it, as Mark Twain quipped, that we are the only animal that blushes, or needs to? Why is it that when we see things as they are, we somehow also know the way things ought to be—or at least we know what they ought not to be? How, if we sense that things are out of joint, can we protest so emphatically and vehemently, even when we cannot cite the standards that allow us to do so? What other beings in the universe are like us with moral and aesthetic notions in these ways?

Life is short, and the day is soon coming when we as individuals will not be here, and for all but very few of us there will be almost no evidence that we have ever been here. So, what does that say about us here and now, and what does it say of our destiny? What other beings are even conscious of such questions? What lies at the heart of this grand paradox of who we humans are?

ONLY DUST BLOWING IN THE WIND?

Last, and far from least, each of our own little individual lives are wonderful too. The unique face that we each have is only the beginning of our uniqueness, and the basics of human living are wonderful in ways that our day-to-day existence rarely notices and, if we are honest, hardly justifies. But is there any rhyme or reason behind it all? Does our individual uniqueness mean nothing? Are we in our brief times on earth just accidents, "dust blowing in the wind" as the song says, the beneficiaries of a dumb, blind stroke of luck? Do we, as painter and atheist Francis Bacon said, just come from one void and go to another, the void before we were born and the void after we die? Were we born just to breathe, eat, sleep, work, talk, laugh, make love, wear out, and die? Is that all there is to our lives? Or is there "something more," something that would be the key to understanding life more positively, and finding life more fulfilling, however short or long, however famous or unknown?

The truth is that we are a generation that has too much to live with and too little to live for. It is therefore time once more for our generation to give such questions the serious thought they deserve. It is not enough simply to live, determinedly or otherwise, without thinking or caring much about life itself. We need to think about ourselves and our world from a big-picture perspective. We need to slow down enough to ponder the wonder of life, and the challenges and predicaments of the world, and ask questions about the meaning of it all. It is time to pay attention to what Socrates famously called the examined life.

("The unexamined life is not worth living," he said as he calmly faced his own execution.) We need to find the meaning behind the mysteries.

FOR THOSE WITH EARS TO HEAR

The good news is that life and the world around us, and whoever and whatever may be behind it all, will not allow us to give up on the questions. They do not allow us to rest completely at ease in the cave. It is not that life and the world are personal in the way we humans are, but that they do not allow us to be fulfilled by views of ourselves that are actually less than we somehow know we are. Are we no more than toolmakers, "naked apes," or selfish genes? Somehow, we humans are never fulfilled looking downward like that. There is always a reaching *upward*. There is too much of us left unsatisfied by such descriptions that do not fit all that we are. (When Plato described the human being as a featherless biped, Diogenes responded by plucking a chicken, throwing it into the assembly, and declaring, "Here is your Platonic man.") We somehow know we are made of more, and we are made for more, so again and again we are restless because we long for something more. Life and the universe therefore refuse to remain silent, and they trigger a thousand questions in us. For those with ears to hear, and for those who dare to pay attention, the universe is alive with sounds and signals to suggest that outside the cave there is a wider world—a world of warmth, color, and brilliance, lit by the reality of the sun and the author of it all.

We may be sternly intent on suppressing wonder and on leading unexamined lives, but the world around us is alive and it never stops speaking to us, telling us about itself and questioning us about our own true selves. To be sure, we are always free to stop our ears, to turn up the volume of our diversions, and to refuse to think or care about what life and the universe are saying. If we are determined and insistent, we can be content with our small worlds, our daily rounds, and our too-easily-settled answers. But the universe keeps on speaking, and its myriad signals, clues, and pointers are there for all who have ears to hear.

This book tells the stories of some who have listened to life and pursued the discovery to which the signals pointed, and it is written for all who are open to that possibility. Listening to such signals of transcendence is only one part, but a vital part, of leading an examined life. It is for those who are not content to remain tone-deaf to wider realities, and who have not fallen for what Friedrich Nietzsche called the acoustic illusion—the fallacy that what we ourselves cannot hear is not objectively there to be heard. I am writing for all who are open to signals that the Hebrew sage called eternity in our hearts and that Wordsworth called intimations of immortality—signals, as he put it, from a world not yet realized.

Do you already "know what you see and hear," in the sense that you have already made up your mind about what there is to be seen and heard, so that you can see and hear nothing else? Or do you "see and hear in order to know," in the sense that you are open to the surprise of new insight and fresh perception? Seeing and hearing only what you know is thinking shackled by the past. Seeing and hearing in order to know are the way of a mind and a heart that are open to a breakthrough and to a future different from both the past and the present.

That we almost all hear such signals is beyond doubt. The stories that follow bear witness to that truth, and they could be multiplied endlessly. But let me be clear. The signals are pointers, and not proofs, and they can be ignored rather than listened to. Arthur Koestler, the Hungarian writer, was one who heard such a signal but never followed through. Indeed, many years after his experience he and his wife killed themselves together in a suicide pact. Yet he was quite clear about the time when he was young and first experienced such an epiphany.

> I was lying on my back under a blue sky on a hill slope in Buda. . . . The paradox of infinity suddenly pierced my brain as if I had been stung by a wasp. . . . The idea that infinity would remain an unsolved riddle was unbearable. The thirst for the absolute is a stigma which marks those unable to find satisfaction in the relative world of the here and now. . . . The infinite as a target was replaced by Utopias of one kind or another.

TO EACH, THEIR OWN SIGNAL

The question to ask after each of these stories is not simply whether we ourselves have heard similar signals. Many have done that. The question is how we have each responded—especially when the censors and the scoffers form so loud a chorus and a cordon around us. What do such signals mean? Are they only a will-o'-the-wisp, leading honest seekers astray into the darkness and the bogs of illusion? Are they only a false dawn that ushers in a day no different and no better than today? Or are they signals pointing to solutions that are solid and to satisfactions that are a delight? What is the truth to which the signals point? Does the search show that there is nothing more to life than our caves and our windowless worlds? Or do the signals, and the stories of those who followed them, point the way to the promise and fulfillment of the something more that encourages us to surpass ourselves and make life more richly satisfying than it is now?

The answer is not for me to spell out here. It is for each reader to decide for herself or himself through search and discovery. Without question, we all hear at times such signals as those we will explore in the coming chapters. But again, the question is what we do with them—our responsibility in responding to them. Are we too shy, too embarrassed to even consider them as signals, to share our experiences with others, and to follow the thrusting logic of their questions, wherever they lead and whatever the cost? Are we afraid of reaching conclusions that might be dismissed as odd, deluded, or out of line with fashionable opinion in our day? In the world of the blind, the one-eyed person always runs the risk of being scoffed at as an idiot.

In Bertolt Brecht's work *Mahagonny*, a brief line has haunted many in his audiences: "something is missing." The question to ask, of course, is whether something is always missing, and life is simply like that—unfulfilling and unfulfillable. Or whether the sense of something missing is an invaluable spur to search for the satisfaction of a longing that needs to be satisfied—and can be.

In the stories that follow, the emphasis will be on the signals that spur the search, rather than the search itself, let alone the discoveries. The focus on the signals as spurs is deliberate. We live in an age in which the overwhelming majority of people appear to be comfortable with their myopia. They are satisfied with the comforts and conveniences of the cave and the windowless world. Our main challenge is to prompt people to think and care sufficiently to begin to ask questions. In each of the stories shared here, the people who followed the signals would all say that their discoveries outshone the importance of the signals by far. Once they had arrived, who cared about the signals? Yet without the signals, they would not have arrived, and they might never have set off on the search. Each signal, then, is small and insignificant in itself, yet titanic in its significance for the whole of life.

In the same way, we can say with certainty that those who close their ears to such signals, for whatever reason, are certain to be losers. In terms of Plato's parable, the closed-minded condemn themselves to serve out their life sentences in their various caves and cells, with no chance of discovering whether the light and freedom of the sun outside are real. Lacking all curiosity, they are content to live in the darkness and never know the truth. But it is time for the signals and the stories to speak for themselves and to let each of us decide for ourselves. There are always choices and consequences in life, and the responsibility to decide them and live with them is always ours.

One truth, however, runs like a thread through the stories. Each signal of transcendence sounds out its own special call. No signal is a signal for everyone to hear, so one person's signal is another person's silence. Be ready, then, for the call that will come to you in your life. Whoever has ears to hear, let him hear.

1

THE LIGHTS OF HOME

Malcolm Muggeridge

F atuous, preposterous, desultory—Malcolm Muggeridge was famous for the way he rolled his favorite words around in his mouth, savoring each one like a gourmand relishing a mouthful before delivering them in his incomparable way of speaking. Behind the rich currency of his speech was not just a love of language but a life rich in experiencing the things of which he spoke. He therefore took seriously only the solid and the proven. All else, including much that others considered solid, he had already weighed and found wanting—fatuous, preposterous, and desultory, in fact, compared with the rocklike realities he sought. On his tombstone are carved three words from John Bunyan that summed up his life and work, *Valiant for Truth*.

To all who had the privilege of knowing Malcolm Muggeridge, he was one of the most celebrated writers, journalists, and satirists of the twentieth century, but far more. He was a small man in stature, but a giant of originality, brilliance, courage, humor, and honesty—and utterly unforgettable.

"An egghead I came into this world," Muggeridge wrote of himself, "and an egghead shall I depart thence." His first memory in life was of walking down a suburban street in someone else's hat—and the rage and heartbreak of that early feeling of displacement never left him. "I have always felt myself, perhaps to an abnormal degree, a stranger in a strange land." It left him, he said, with "the related feeling that the whole life of action, one's own and the society's or civilization's to which one happened to belong, is theater; a lurid melodrama or soap-opera with history for its theme."

The outcome for Muggeridge's view of life was profound. In his introduction to his book *The Thirties*, written from an army hut as World War II broke out, he confessed that he was unable to believe in the validity or permanence of any form of authority. "Crowns and miters seem to have been made of tinsel, ceremonial robes to have been procured in theatrical costumiers, what passes for great oratory to have been mugged up from the worst of Shakespeare." The trouble was that, in the eyes of others, such a disposition made him appear "ostensibly irreverent, pessimistic, disloyal, and—the commonest accusation—destructive in attitude of mind."

The same feeling gave Muggeridge the viewpoint of a maverick and the humor of a satirist, but it also formed a stubborn independence that never fell prey to fashion or consensus. He became the much-loved and much-loathed editor of *Punch,* Britain's humor magazine. No one was more impatient with humbug, no one had a keener eye for the absurdity of human pretensions, and no one could capture the emptiness of the carnival of human affairs like he did—but all with a passion for truth and without a shred of cynicism. As one biographer wrote, and he himself admitted, Muggeridge always knew what he disbelieved before he knew what he believed. He had sorted through things, discarding the flimsy for the solid, the boring and predictable for that which was fresh and incongruous but true.

Muggeridge described his four years at Cambridge University as "the most futile and dismal of my whole life." Three years in India, perhaps the most religious country in the world, shattered any belief he had in religion. Two years in Stalin's Russia, to which he had gone as a fervent, young, utopian socialist, left his political idealism in ruins. (He was the first voice to report and denounce the horrors of Stalin's induced famines in Ukraine that starved more than four million people between 1922 and 1930.) Looking down from his editorial perch at the *Manchester Guardian*, he summed up the "dismal Thirties" as "a decade which began with the illusion of progress without tears and ended up in the reality of tears without progress." So much for the assured answers of education, religion, politics, and history. In a few short years he had seen through them all.

Muggeridge's reporting from the Soviet Union was remarkable for its bravery. History was to vindicate him fully, though he did not live to see the collapse of the USSR. At the time, his report triggered a hail of denunciations from all sides, including from intellectuals such as George Bernard Shaw, who claimed to have seen overflowing Soviet granaries and apple-cheeked maids working at them. Muggeridge described the *New York Times* correspondent, who received a Pulitzer Prize for his positive reports on Stalin, as "the greatest liar I have ever met." Throughout the decade, he felt he was observing the extraordinary fact that "the sun seemed to be setting on the Empire on which it never set." Walking through London in the dark days of the blitz with his friend Graham Greene, "I felt I was at the last bonfire of the last remains of our derelict civilization." Paraphrasing Rudyard

Kipling, he would say, "I saw the sunset ere most men saw the dawn."

The turning point for Muggeridge was the night he intended to commit suicide in Africa in 1943. As he tells the story in his memoir, *Chronicles of Wasted Time*, he was turned down when he tried to enlist in the army in World War II. Instead, he was seconded to the embryonic Intelligence Corps, but sent to Lourenço Marques in Mozambique, far from any action that was either interesting or important. He was given the task of monitoring German shipping. Increasingly it seemed that his life amounted to a dire schooling in progressive disillusionment. "It was now that the absurdity, the futility, the degradation of how I had been living seized me with irresistible force."

One night, Muggeridge lay on his bed

full of stale liquor and despair; alone in the house, and as it seemed, utterly alone, not just in Lourenço Marques, in Africa, in the world. Alone in the universe, in eternity, with no glimmer of light in the prevailing blackness; no human voice I could hope to hear, or human heart I could hope to reach, no God to whom I could turn, or Savior to take my hand.

He had no one and nothing to turn to. Suddenly the thought struck him. "Deprived of war's only solace—death, given and received, it came into my mind that there was, after all, one death I could still procure. My own. I decided to kill myself."

It was before the day of barbiturates, but, Muggeridge said, drowning would look like an accident, which would be better for his family. Driving six miles out of the small Mozambique town, he found a deserted beach, undressed and swam out into the cold, dark water. But suddenly he stopped. His last anguished thoughts were of his wife, Kitty, back in England. Glancing back as he swam, he had seen the lights of Peter's Café and the Costa da Sol. He suddenly saw them as he had never seen them before, and they stopped him in his tracks. "They were the lights of the world; they were the lights of my home, my habitat, where I belonged. I must reach them. There followed an overwhelming joy such as I had never experienced before; an ecstasy."

He swam back. He would still always see the sunset before others saw the dawn. He would still always feel he was a stranger in a strange land, but the world was no longer entirely foreign. The lights of home had blinked to him in the darkness. In a world of absurdity and pomposity, there was hope, and he had to find its true source.

Was this a conversion experience for Muggeridge? Not at all. He would have snorted at the thought. It was years before he came to any satisfying conclusions about faith and life. But that night was the turning point. The experience, he wrote, was a "kind of spiritual adolescence, whereby, thenceforth, all my values and pursuits and hopes were going to undergo a total transformation." Deliberately or not, his words echoed Plato's parable of the cave. "In a tiny dungeon of the ego, chained and manacled, I had glimpsed a glimmer of light coming in through a barred window high above me." Having seen that glimmer of light, he threw himself into the quest to follow where it led.

Muggeridge never lost his sense of being out of place in the world. He never shook off the feeling that he was a stranger in a strange land. Indeed, he came to see how warranted that feeling is, and should be, for human beings. Yet if this world is not our home, then it is our duty to see through its flimsiness, its pretensions, and its pomposities. Perhaps we were made for somewhere else, and for something more. But was there such a place, or was it a mirage? Like a flash in the darkness of the absurdity all around, the lights of the little café had signaled home and hope. And suddenly and intuitively, he responded to the signal by turning around in the water and heading back to the shore. His action was a quest for home, a bid for life and purpose and for the reason for it all—if there was a reason.

Malcolm Muggeridge was a long way from believing in anything, but the flash that spelled home was the signal of transcendence that stopped him from ending his life, turned him around, and made him a seeker. Could there be life and sunshine outside the cave? He had seen a glimpse of the sun from his cell, and that was enough to spur him to want to find out if there was a world outside.

A faith, a philosophy of life, or a view of life and the world, provides us with three things: meaning, belonging, and a story line. It helps us make sense of life. It gives us security in our world. And it unfolds the direction and purpose of our destiny on earth. It was the second of these that arrested Muggeridge. The lights of the little café had signaled and called to his heart that, across the wasteland of the earth, there was home. The signal of transcendence was an intuition, and the intuition was an invitation, and Muggeridge set out at once to find whether the signal led anywhere, and whether the home at the journey's end was real or an illusion.

The impact of a signal of transcendence is all important. It creates a seeker and shapes the direction of his or her search. When a signal breaks in, life raises a question that cannot be answered within a person's present frame of meaning. A seeker is born. Seekers are jolted into inquiring further than they have ever looked or thought before. The signal is the making of a seeker.

Not merely questioned, but called into question, people who hear a signal somehow know in their hearts that they are responsible to answer the question. They are being addressed as responsible human beings, humans not only able to respond but unable to ignore the challenge to respond. It is the very thrust and intensity of the question that creates the seeker and directs the course of the search.

Years later, Malcolm Muggeridge, in his own words, "rediscovered Jesus" and became a Christian—through the influence of friends, such as the reformer Lord Pakenham, and great saints, such as Mother Teresa. It was Muggeridge who brought the little saint of the Calcutta poor to the world's attention through his television documentary *Something Beautiful for God*. But his journey had begun all those years earlier, in the dark waters off the coast of Africa, when the signal of transcendence punctured his overwhelming sense of estrangement and futility, pointing him toward home.

Home and "a place for us"—there is immense power in the signal that points toward home and belonging. There is no hearth like the hearth of home, as the Irish saying goes. But remember that each signal of transcendence sounds out its own special call. No signal is a signal for everyone to hear, so one person's signal is another person's silence. Be ready, then, for the call that comes to you in your own life. Whoever has ears to hear, let him hear.

2

EVERY MOTHER'S COMFORT

Peter Berger

A s the dark menace of Hitler lowered over Germany in the 1930s, Martin Buber, the eminent Jewish philosopher, became concerned for his nine- and eleven-year old grand-daughters who were living with him and his wife. He was not concerned for himself, though his own freedom to speak and publish was steadily curtailed, but the young girls were experiencing the threat differently. At their school, they were no longer addressed by name, but simply as "You there," and the harshness of the changes was unsettling their world.

In response, Buber wrote an article titled "Die Kinder" (The Children).

Children experience what happens and keep silent, but in the night they groan in their dreams, awaken, and stare into the darkness: The world has become unreliable. A child had a friend: the friend was taken for granted as the sunlight. Now the friend suddenly looks at him strangely, the corners of his mouth mock him: Surely you didn't imagine that I really cared about you? A child had a teacher, a certain one among all others. He knew that this person existed, so everything was alright. Now the teacher no longer has a voice when he speaks to him. . . . What has happened? A child knows many things, but he still doesn't know how it all fits together.

The urgent need, Buber argued, was for the Jews to rebuild trust for their children as a matter of spiritual resistance.

For its spirit to grow, a child needs what is constant, what is dependable. There must be something that does not fail. The home is not enough; the world must be part of it. What has happened to this world? The familiar smile had turned into a scowl. I know nothing else but this: to make something unshakable visible in the child's world. . . . It is up to us to make the world reliable again for the children. It depends on us where we can say to them and ourselves, "Don't worry, Mother is here."

THERE IS NO ONE ALIVE WHO DID NOT HAVE A MOTHER

We are all here on earth because of our mothers. No single human being who has ever lived did not have a mother. Peter Berger's opening example of a signal of transcendence is both a deep reflection on life and a moving tribute to all the mothers of the world. We may admire prominent and gifted people, such as Malcolm Muggeridge and the others who will come in these stories. But they are unusual people. We admire them for their gifts and their achievements, and we wish we could be like them, though in certain key ways, they are not like us and we will never be like them. But in fact we are all special to each other because no two human beings are exactly alike, just as no two faces are exactly alike.

Thus the signals of transcendence speak to all of us, because they speak to us as human beings and not only to special people. And what is more elemental and universal, down the centuries and across the continents, than a mother's reassurance to an anxious child in the night? The image of a mother cradling her child is "a universally understood human icon," Berger says. "Someone once observed that every new mother is in a morally privileged position. She knows exactly what God wants her to do. That is, of course, to take care of her child." That reassurance was exactly what Martin Buber and his wife wanted for their grand-daughters in the unsettled days in Germany in the 1930s.

"A child wakes up in the night, perhaps from a bad dream, and finds himself surrounded by darkness, beset by nameless threats. At such a moment the contours of trusted reality are blurred or invisible, and in the terror of incipient chaos the child cries out for his mother." It is not an exaggeration, Berger says, that at that moment the mother is being called on as the grand protector of order and safety. She, and she alone, has the power to expel the darkness, banish the terror, and restore the familiar safety of the world. For the poet W. H. Auden, the human race itself is no more than "children afraid of the night."

Berger continues,

And, of course, any good mother will do just that. She will take the child and cradle him in the timeless gesture of the Magna Mater who became our Madonna. She will turn on the lamp, perhaps, which will encircle the scene with a warm glow of reassuring light. She will speak or sing to the child, and the content of this communication will invariably be the same—"Don't be afraid—Everything is in order. Everything is all right." If all goes well, the child will be reassured, his trust in reality recovered, and in this trust he will return to sleep.

Could there be any scene more natural, unexceptional, and common—whether the mother is Jewish, Scottish, Chinese, or Brazilian, a first-century matron in Rome, a nineteenth-century ballet dancer in Paris, or a high school teacher in the American Midwest? The Middle Eastern oil lamp may have been replaced by a medieval candle and then by an electric light. And the lullaby may be an impromptu cooing or rise to the beauty of a Brahms's lullaby. But the scene and the response are the same. We all have had mothers, and without them we would not be alive. We can all sense the human terror at the prospect of chaos, and the way a mother's reassurance returns the world to protective safety. "Don't worry. Mother is here. Everything is all right."

IS THE ASSURANCE TRUE?

Yet go a little deeper, Berger probes. Think about what the mother has said. "Everything is okay. Everything is all right." At one level, that is a very ordinary statement, every mother's loving reassurance. But at another level it raises far from ordinary questions. How can the mother say that? Is the mother honest or lying? For the truth is that everything is not all right. There are things in the world that are badly wrong, as the child will discover sooner or later, including the fact that both the mother and the child will die in the end. Does that mean, then, that the mother's words are actually a lie unless there is reason to be able to trust in existence as it is, in spite of the contradictions existence appears to have? After all, if for whatever reason we cannot have confidence in the final goodness and safety of the universe, then the mother is lying—though as Berger is quick to add, "lying out of love, to be sure."

In other words, Berger continues, the simple words of any mother's reassurance in the night are a signal of transcendence. Why? "Because the reassurance, transcending the immediate two individuals and their situation, implies a statement about reality as such." But is this intuition about the safety of ultimate reality true? How do we know, and how can we find out? Might it not be better to understand the motive for telling the lie, forgive the ultimate inaccuracy, and stick with the lie to bring the immediate comfort a child needs?

Berger explains his point more prosaically. Mothers (and fathers) are world builders and world protectors for their children. Parents are in the business of providing order, meaning, and stability for their families. If they are successful, they are launching into life new members of the human race with a sure sense of identity and clear sense of purpose. Such a sense of order is essential for both individuals and societies. Parents naturally pass on the particular understanding of order that their own society adheres to, but deeper than that, parents are the prime source of order itself. As Berger explains, "The formula can, without in any way violating it, be translated into a statement of cosmic scope— 'Have trust in being.' . . . Put differently, at the very center of the process of becoming fully human, at the core of *humanitas*, we find an experience of trust in the order of reality. Is this experience an illusion? Is the individual who represents it a liar?"

At one level, the answer has to be that if reality goes no wider than the world we experience through our five senses, then the claim is false and the assurance is a lie. No one can look around the world of today, with its conflicts, wars, oppressions, poverty, hunger, disease, prejudices, inequalities, and injustices, and pronounce it "all right." Plainly the world for Martin Buber, his granddaughters, and all their fellow Jews was far from right. It was terribly wrong. Berger continues, "The world that the child is being told to trust is the same world in which he will eventually die. If there is no other world, then the ultimate truth about this one is that eventually it will kill the child as it will kill his mother." Again, Berger hastens to add, that does not detract from the mother's love—"it would even give this love a quality of tragic heroism. Nevertheless, the final truth would not be love but terror, not light but darkness." Then the best we could offer our children is a "merciful illusion," and the last word on life would be Freud's. Belief in the ultimate goodness of existence is a projection and wish fulfillment. Faith is only fantasy, and the mature person must face the universe as it is with the open-eyed courage of a stoic like Marcus Aurelius.

Berger emphasizes that his comments are not moral judgments. No one is condemning the mother for her false declaration or arguing that atheists cannot be wonderful parents—though, he adds, "it is not without interest that there have been atheists who have rejected parenthood for exactly these reasons." (The Hungarian novelist Arthur Koestler was an outspoken example. He refused to bring children into the world.) But the logic of the signal is philosophical rather than moral. The instinctive human reassurance, in resorting to claims for the ultimate goodness of existence, punctures the view of the world bound by the five senses alone (the world without windows of the atheist and secularist). And it points toward higher, wider, deeper possibilities that would have to be true if the reassurance is in fact warranted.

The characteristic double thrust of a signal of transcendence, with both a contradiction and a desire, is clear in this case. The heartfelt genuineness of the mother's reassurance contradicts the secularist view, according to which the reassurance is ultimately a lie. Things in the world are not finally all right. But while the clear desire for a better view is strong and natural, that by itself does not make it true. Feuerbach, Marx, and Freud may still be right, and the trust in ultimate existence that lies behind the reassurance may be only a projection or a matter of wish fulfillment. Hence the importance of the search required of those who wish to be true to Socrates's examined life.

Our focus here, however, is on the signals, and a full discussion of the search is beyond the scope of this book. But the overall logic is clear. The signal of transcendence sounds out and spurs the search. The seeker launches out on a quest to discover whether there are grounds for such faith and meaning. And, through the search, the seeker settles the argument one way or another.

"UNMOVED MOVER" OR MOST-MOVED MOVER?

Berger's reflection on reassurance and the need for "order" sounds most powerfully on the personal level. "Every parent," he says, "(or, at any rate, every parent who loves his child) takes upon himself the representation of a universe that is ultimately ordered and ultimately trustworthy." The trouble is, such ultimate trustworthiness cannot be found within a worldview that goes no higher and wider than the world in which we are born, we live, and we will die—which means people must pay attention to the signal, and have the courage to leave the cave and its shadows, and set off to search for something better, even if no one else wishes to hear what they hear or agree with what they find.

Berger's comments struck a deep chord in me because of my own experience. I was born in war-torn China, at a time when seventeen million Chinese were killed in the Japanese invasion, which climaxed in the brutal and horrendous rape of Nanking. At one point, our family was caught in a catastrophic famine caused by locusts and the heartlessness of the Nationalist government. Five million people in our province, Henan, died in three months, including my older and younger brothers. My mother, who was a surgeon, could do nothing. There was no food and no medicine to be had. Beside the hunger and disease, horrors, such as cannibalism and parents selling their children for the next meal, stalked the land. We later moved to the southern capital Nanking, where we witnessed the climax of the Chinese revolution and the opening years of repression and the reign of terror.

My first ten years, to put it gently, were years of chaos, disorder, terror, fear, death, suffering, war, revolution, and loss—history in concentrated form. Everything was not all right. Everything was often all wrong. Yet in spite of everything, my parents had come to a sure faith in God. They knew that the situation was all wrong, and why; they knew that it should have been otherwise, yet they could still trust in God and in the ultimate goodness of things. Not once in those dark years did I ever see my father or mother waver in their own faith and in their calm reassurance to me. "God is greater than all. God can be trusted in all situations. Have faith in God. Have no fear. Everything will be all right."

My parents' faith was no leap in the dark. It was a rational and warranted faith, the outcome of their own search and conviction. It went beyond reason, because they were more than reason, but it was never against reason. Their faith gave them rock-solid grounds for trusting in the ultimate goodness of life and existence, despite the horror and sorrow of the immediate situation. The final reality behind the universe is God, who is love, and who has a great heart for humans whom he has created in his own image. If God is for us, then fate, chance, necessity, entropy, war, famine, heartlessness, and death do not have the last word on life. As Lincoln concluded in the horror of the carnage of the American Civil War, "The will of God prevails."

History, as historians have said, may appear to be like a grand Rorschach test. Life as we humans experience it may be a chaotic jumble of good and bad, beauty and brokenness, delights, disappointments, and disasters. And as we know well, our individual wills and desires clash repeatedly with the contrary wills and desires of others. Thus in order to live well and make sense of the crazy-quilt confusion of experiences, we have to discover a pattern of meaning in the jumble of dots. We do this through the ultimate beliefs that we each hold to be true, which for better or worse promise to show us the final meaning of it all.

Each person who hears the signal, then, has to search for the answer that the signal points to, and find it for themselves. We each have to ask, what is the final meaning of it all? Who or what is the ultimate reality behind everything? What will have the last word on our lives? Is life only "a tale told by an idiot," as Shakespeare says in *Macbeth*? Is it merely a "trash bag of random coincidences torn open in a wind," as Joseph Heller wrote? Will the last word on our lives be the iron hand of fate, as so many of the ancients believed, and as happened to the hapless Oedipus? Will it be chance, necessity, determinism, karma, or our stars?

There are many different answers to these questions. They could all be false, but with so many differing claims they cannot all be true. Which one is true is for the seeker to assess and judge. But one fact is beyond question. The Jewish and Christian view stands in strong contrast to the bleak alternatives. Behind our little daily lives, behind the unstoppable torrents of history, and behind the universe itself, is God who has created us in his image, who loves us, and who has a heart for us. Is God the "Unmoved Mover" of Aristotle? Absolutely not, Rabbi Abraham Joshua Heschel protested: God is the "most moved mover."

Berger's own personal response was clear. All the reassurance of all the world's mothers can only be justified if the natural world is not the only world, "but only the foreground of another world in which love is not annihilated in death, and in which, therefore the trust in the power of love to banish chaos is justified." As a person of deep faith himself, he wrote, "Thus man's ordering propensity implies a transcendent order, and each ordering gesture is a signal of transcendence. The parental role is not based on a loving lie. On the contrary, it is a witness to the ultimate truth of man's situation in reality."

Order, safety, and protection—the signal that points toward there being such assurance in existence strikes a chord deep in most of our hearts. But remember once again that each signal of transcendence sounds out its own special call. No signal is a signal for everyone to hear, so one person's signal is another person's silence. Be ready, then, for the call that comes to you in your life. Whoever has ears to hear, let him hear.

3

CRIES TO HEAVEN,
CRIES FOR HELL

W. H. Auden

W. H. Auden was one of the greatest English-speaking poets of the twentieth century, and scathingly dismissive of literary biographers. "Biographies of writers," he declared toward the end of his life, "are always superfluous and usually in bad taste. A writer is a maker, not a man of action. . . . His private life is, or should be, of no concern to anybody except himself, his family, and his friends." Auden dismissed such biographers as "gossip writers and voyeurs, calling themselves scholars." He went so far as to propose that writers publish their work anonymously. Then readers could concentrate on their writing rather than the writer. When Auden died in 1973, he stated in his will that his friends should burn his letters in order to "make a biography impossible."

But to paraphrase Shakespeare, the gentleman doth protest too much. Or to paraphrase Freud, Auden's slip was showing. Nietzsche may have been exaggerating when he said that all philosophy is biography, but only by a little. Even if philosophy or poetry is not reducible to biography, the link between a writer's life and work is too close to sever, and no one is a clearer example than W. H. Auden—as in his experience of the signal of transcendence that turned his life around and transformed the poet into an active seeker.

KILL THEM!

On September 1, 1939, Hitler invaded Poland, and the Second World War began. Having moved to New York in January to escape the lowering storm clouds, Auden wrote a poem named after the date. "I sit in one of the dives / On Fifty Second Street," he began, referring to the ending of "a low dishonest decade." He was already a young hero as a poet when he came to America. He was also known as an atheist, a left-wing socialist, a homosexual, and a veteran of the Spanish Civil War, in which he had volunteered on the Republican side for seven weeks. Along with his Oxford contemporaries Stephen Spender and Cecil Day-Lewis, he was one of the most influential English-speaking poets of his age. Many considered him a prophet for his generation. There was little in his life that would draw him to any religious belief, and what happened surprised even some of his closest friends.

When Auden arrived in the United States with Christopher Isherwood in January 1939, he was not religious, and he hadn't been since he was thirteen at Gresham's School in England. Both his grandfathers had been clergymen, but he described the religion he encountered at boarding school as "nothing but vague uplift, as flat as an old bottle of soda water." "At thirteen," he wrote, "I was confirmed. To say that shortly afterwards I lost my faith would be melodramatic and false. I simply lost interest." From then on, reinforced by his time as an undergraduate at

Christ Church, Oxford, he was convinced that "people only love God when no one else will love them." Needless to say, the times in which he lived were hardly conducive to faith. Malcolm Muggeridge had described the thirties as a "dismal decade." Auden called it the "low dishonest decade."

Two experiences, however, jolted Auden into rethinking. The first had come earlier in 1933, when he was a schoolmaster at the Downs School in the Malvern Hills. Sitting with three fellow teachers one day, he was suddenly overwhelmed by the sense that all their existence somehow had infinite value and that he loved them for themselves. But why? The flooding sense of love did not last long, and he put the experience behind him. Years later he described what had happened as a "Vision of Agape" (Love).

The second and deeper experience was more decisive. It happened in New York two months after Auden had written the poem "September 1, 1939." There was no television in those days, so he used to keep in touch with news from Europe by listening to the radio, and by attending his local cinema and watching the weekly documentary news. One weekend he went to a cinema in Yorkville on the Upper East Side of Manhattan, near where he had lived when he first arrived. It was still largely a German-speaking area. The United States had not entered the war at that stage, so he found himself, an Englishman, sitting in the darkness with a theater full of Germans openly supporting the other side.

Auden had read a review of the film, which rather unusually focused on the audience and not just the film, but he was not prepared for the audience response he met. The film was *Sieg im Poland*, a documentary of the Nazi invasion and conquest of Poland. It was graphic. Hitler's SS storm troopers were bayoneting women and children, and members of the audience cried out in support of their fellow countrymen, "Kill the Poles! Kill them!"

Auden froze in his seat. He was horrified. "I wondered then, why I reacted as I did against the denial of every humanistic value." His answer, he said, turned him into a seeker. His philosophy of life at the time was a broad mix of liberal-socialist-democratic opinions, following his earlier intellectual odyssey through the dogmas of Sigmund Freud and Karl Marx. But one thread had always linked his successive convictions—a belief in the natural goodness of humankind. Like many of his generation, he firmly believed that the solution to the world's problems lay in politics, education, or psychology. He also believed that if the problems were addressed constructively, the world could be happy because humanity was essentially good. As the war broke out, he had been determined to "show an affirming flame" and make some stand for freedom. As he put it in the closing lines of his poem "September 1, 1939," "All I have is a voice / To undo the folded lie."

Suddenly, however, as Auden watched the SS savagery and heard the brutal response of the audience, he knew he had been quite wrong. First, with everything in him he knew intuitively and beyond any doubt that he was looking at absolute evil. Second, he knew that such evil must be judged and condemned absolutely. There had to be a reason why Hitler was "utterly wrong." Profoundly shaken, Auden reflected on this experience. Just as in the nineteenth century, Dostoyevsky's belief in the goodness of the Russian peasant had been shattered by the peasant depravity he encountered in Siberia, so Auden's facile confidence in human goodness had collapsed like a pricked balloon.

At the very end of the nineteenth century, in his book *Social Statics*, Herbert Spencer had actually written, "evil perpetually tends to disappear. . . . Progress, therefore, is not an accident but a necessity. Evil and immorality must surely disappear; man must surely become perfect." It was the perfect expression of the simple, easygoing optimism of the eighteenth-century Enlightenment, but after the Great War it was ludicrous and after World War II and the Nazi death camps, it was unthinkable. William Golding admitted the impossibility, explaining why he had written his novel *Lord of the Flies,*

> Before the second world war I believed in the perfectibility of man . . . but after the war I did not because I was unable to. I had discovered what one man could do to another. . . . I must say that anyone who moved through those years without understanding that man produces evil as a bee produces honey must have been blind or wrong in the head.

ABSOLUTELY WRONG, BUT WHY?

For Auden, the experience thrust on him two issues that were troubling for what he believed—how to account for the undeniable evil he had encountered, and how to justify condemning it with an unconditional and absolute judgment. After all, for educated people like him there were no absolutes of any kind in his universe. (A favorite phrase of William James was "Damn the absolute!" and in James Joyce's *A Portrait of the Artist as a Young Man,* Stephen Dedalus keeps repeating his mantra, "The Absolute is dead.") To judge anything absolutely was naive and unthinkable, the sort of thing done only by "the great unwashed." Following Nietzsche, all self-respecting philosophers had abandoned absolute judgments. God was dead and truth was dead, and all that was left was relativism (your truth / my truth or his truth /

her truth) and emotivism ("what I feel is good is good" and "what I feel is bad is bad"). Long before the day of political correctness, psychologists had thrown over absolutes in favor of nonjudgmental tolerance and acceptance. "Thou shalt not judge" was the eleventh commandment.

Auden pressed his concerns on his friends. "The English intellectuals who now cry to Heaven against the evil incarnated in Hitler have no Heaven to cry to," he told one friend. It was clear to him that liberalism had a fatal flaw. "The whole trend of liberal thought," he wrote the next year, "has been to undermine faith in the absolute. . . . It has tried to make reason the judge. . . . But since life is a changing process . . . the attempt to find a humanistic basis of keeping a promise works logically with the conclusion, 'I can break it whenever I feel convenient.'" He pressed the point in an interview in the *Observer*, "Unless one is prepared to take a relativist view that all morals are a matter of personal taste, one could hardly avoid asking the question: 'If, as I am convinced, the Nazis are wrong and we are right, what is it that validates our values and invalidates theirs?'" For those who were relativists, it was impossible to make moral judgments on the Nazis. "Were not the Nazis merely being true to their own nature, to all our natures?"

The only remedy when facing such malignant evil, Auden concluded, was to renew "faith in the absolute." It was "the only possible ground for moral judgment." Or as he posed the challenge in a poem written soon after his visit to the Yorkville cinema: "Either we serve the unconditional," or some Hitlerian monster will force us to see things his way. Auden had entered the cinema an atheist and left it a seeker after an unconditional absolute. He started attending church the next year and became a lifelong Christian.

ARGUMENT FROM DAMNATION

Auden's experience once again demonstrates the double-barreled logic of a signal of transcendence. Its message acted as a contradiction and a desire. It punctured the adequacy of what he had believed, and it pointed toward a different and deeper answer that, if found to be true, would be surer, richer, and more adequate than what he had believed until then.

Auden's intuitive and absolute judgment of evil is revealing. Not so long ago, it was fashionable to be entirely nonjudgmental, but the truth is that not to judge at all is quite impossible. We can hardly last five minutes, let alone five days, without judging someone or something as wrong—and meaning it. And worse still, not to judge is unethical, for a failure to call evil "evil" is to compound evil with evil. We may say that God is dead and everything is permitted, but it turns out that lots of things are impermissible, and we object to them. We may say that everything is relative, but the way we behave shows that we think some things are absolutely wrong, and there is no question about it.

It is obvious, too, that we make such judgments long before we are taught to, or taught anything. What is more natural and more common than a small child's "That's not fair!" Children may grow up to be told by college professors that there is no such thing as objective truth and that nothing is absolutely right or wrong, but that is not the way that they, or we, or even the professor, behave. Woe betide the child or adult who cheats us out of anything we consider ours. The abstract ideal of what is just and fair may be vague and arguable, but the raw fact of what is unfair is real, immediate, and something to stand up for with all the passion we can muster.

Peter Berger calls this intuitive reasoning the "argument from damnation," though by "argument" he meant a pointer and not a proof. He illustrated its logic from the Nuremberg trials of the Nazi war criminals. Much had been written, he said, on questions such as "How can such things have been done by human beings?" and on the philosophical and legal basis of the Nuremberg judgments. His concern was to focus on the fact that there was no hesitation in condemning Nazi officers at Nuremberg or Adolf Eichmann at his trial in Jerusalem. The Nazis had committed "legal crimes," in that they were under orders, they were within the laws of their own country, and what they did would have never been condemned if they had won. Was Nuremberg only "victor's justice" then? No, the Allies and Berger responded. The Nazis had committed "crimes against humanity" and condemnation "was an absolute and compelling necessity." Indeed, "a refusal to condemn in absolute terms would appear to offer prima facie evidence not only of a profound failure in the understanding of justice, but more profoundly of a fatal impairment of *humanitas*."

But on what basis? Justice Robert Jackson, the American prosecutor at the Nuremberg trials, stated: "The wrongs which we seek to condemn and punish have been so calculated, so malignant, and so devastating, that civilization cannot afford their being ignored because it cannot survive their being repeated." But Jackson was reaching for the unreachable. "Never again" has since become "again and again," so preventing repetition is clearly an inadequate condemnation. But how can "crimes against humanity" be condemned adequately?

Berger's description of such judgments converges with Auden's. "There are certain deeds that cry out to heaven. These deeds are not only an outrage to our moral sense, they seem to violate a fundamental awareness of the constitution of our humanity. In this way, these deeds are not only evil, but *monstrously* evil." We therefore "suspend relativizations." We do not, and we know we cannot, excuse the Nazis because they come from a different culture and were brought up in a different background than ourselves. No. Absolutely not. What the Nazis did was evil, absolutely evil. Period. Full stop.

This condemnation, Berger continues, contains two steps. First, it punctures our previous thinking. We know that "our condemnation is certain and absolute. It does not permit modification or doubt, and it is made in the conviction that it applies to all times and to all men as well as to the perpetrator or putative perpetrator of the particular deed." In other words, we reject all notions of relative truths and give the condemnation a necessary and universal status even though we could not provide the theoretical justification for doing so. Second, the condemnation points beyond our previous thinking. "Either we deny that there is here anything that can be called truth—a choice that would make us deny what we experience most profoundly as our own being; or we must look beyond the realm of our 'natural' experience for a validation of our certainty."

Such intuitive condemnations commonly go beyond the here and now. Indeed, Berger says, "Deeds that cry out to heaven also cry out for hell." Many people pronounced that "hanging is not enough" for Eichmann—which of course raised the question of what punishment would have been enough.

> No human punishment is "enough" in the case of deeds as monstrous as these. . . . These are deeds that demand not only condemnation, but *damnation* in the full religious

meaning of the word—that is, the doer not only puts himself outside the community of men; he also separates himself in a final way from a moral order that transcends the human community, and thus invokes a retribution that is more than human.

A powerful argument for God, Winston Churchill once growled, "was the existence of Lenin and Trotsky, for whom a hell was needed."

Is there anything to vindicate such judgments—whether W. H. Auden's in the cinema, the Allied judges at Nuremberg, or the spectators of the Eichmann trial? Ask yourself that the next time you make a strong judgment or argue that something is absolutely wrong. What are you assuming in that judgment? Was there anything to vindicate Malcolm Muggeridge's glimpse of home, or the mother's reassurance in the night? That is for the search and the searcher to decide, but the role of the signal is clear, though now over. Fairness in the face of wrong, justice, condemnation, and even damnation in the face of evil, all resonate powerfully and naturally in the human heart, and also powerful is the signal of transcendence that points beyond them.

But remember once again that each signal of transcendence sounds out its own special call. No signal is a signal for everyone to hear, so one person's signal is another person's silence. Be ready, then, for the call that comes to you in your life. Whoever has ears to hear, let him hear.

4

HEART-CRACKING GOODNESS

Philip Hallie

P hilip Hallie was a scholar and an author, and unlike many of the others in these stories, he was neither a celebrity nor well known. Yet the signal of transcendence that transformed his life is the perfect sequel to the experience of W. H. Auden. Face to face with evil, and battling with suicidal despair, his heart was cracked open, not by evil but by goodness. Hallie grew up in a tenement in one of the toughest neighborhoods of Chicago—in a building that he and his brother called "the Cockroach Building." As a boy, he saw the gangster John Dillinger shot, killed, and carted away on his block. Neighborhood bullies beat him up because he was Jewish. He escaped the worst, he said, through a combination of bookishness, school, and an inner-city Christian mission that was close to his home.

Hallie's early years left him with a residual sense that the world was cruel, dangerous, and arbitrary. His experience as an artillery officer in World War II reinforced those feelings exponentially, and after the war he sought refuge in the quieter world of the academy. Graduating from Grinnell College, Iowa, he did graduate work at Harvard and Oxford, and then settled down to teach philosophy and ethics at Wesleyan University in Middletown, Connecticut, where he taught for thirty-two years.

THE ENTRANCE FEE TO HELL

Seeking to make the most of his own experience as a Jew, Hallie set out to become a student of the Holocaust and a specialist on Nazi cruelty. His 1969 book *The Paradox of Cruelty* was highly acclaimed. It was an unflinching account of cruelty of the doctors in the death camps; his intense immersion in the subject—allied with his childhood and wartime experiences, and compounded by his philosophical skepticism—plunged him into deep depression. Neither his family nor his friends could help him shake his sense of despair.

One April evening after his first book came out, Hallie found himself "feeling angry and frightened," and knowing he had to get away from his family. "I was angering and frightening them." He thought he would walk off his mood by walking the mile to his office, but when he got there he felt no better. For more than a month he had been feeling a mixture of fear, bitterness, and fury, and he had not been sleeping much. Sometimes when he was talking to students he would find himself trembling with rage. Early in the walk it had crossed his mind that if he killed himself, his strong Italian wife could well pick up the pieces for his family.

When Hallie reached his office, he was even more miserable than when he set out. His mood had worsened as if he was being sucked down into a bog. "During my walk," he said, "I had thought about a man in a white smock bending over a metal table with a Gypsy or Jewish child on it, cutting off a toe or finger or ear without anesthesia. I wanted to tear the head off the man, and

I wanted to pick up the child and run with him or her out of the death camp. But I could do nothing."

For months Hallie had been studying the torturing and killing of children in the Nazi concentration camps, and again and again he had dwelt on the terrible imbalance of power between the victimizers and the victims. Suddenly it struck him that

> you cannot go down into hell with impunity. You must pay an entrance fee and an exit fee too. I had found myself consciously imitating the victimizers by yearning to victimize them. . . . But the deepest torture I experienced was the shame I felt for my occasional objectivity. Sometimes as I studied the records, the reports, the photographs, the letters, I found myself consciously imitating those monsters who could watch all this without a qualm.

In the course of fifty years, Hallie went on, "I had discovered that I tended to become fascinated by what I was fascinated by. . . . Now I was staring into the face of cruelty and becoming cruelty itself."

AWASH WITH TEARS

As Hallie sat at his desk, the residue of his hope ebbed away until not a shred was left. He turned his chair and looked at the rows of books on his shelves. They represented his years of study and research. Together they documented evil, but not a single one provided any answer to the evil. It appeared that only sheer force could right the wrong and prevail over the powerful smashing the weak. But that was the problem: might always overcame right, and might was on the side of the wrong. If he had ever come across a sliver of hope, it was the French Resistance. It "had always been a tonic to me." So in a mood of ultimate despair, he reached out his hand to a section of books on France and the Resistance, and opened an essay in a booklet he had never read before, the story of a little town he had never heard of before—Le Chambon-sur-Lignon in south-central France.

"By the time I had glanced at a few paragraphs," Hallie said, "I knew why I had not heard about the town: It was a center of *non-violent* resistance against the Nazis and the army had taught me only about violent resistance. When I got to the bottom of the third page of the article my cheeks started itching, and when I reached up to scratch them I found that they were covered with tears—my cheeks were awash with them. For a moment I thought that the tears came from my despair and my near in-sanity. Then I realized that the itching had started when I began to read about two boxy khaki-colored buses coming into the gray granite square of a French mountain village"—they were the Vichy police coming to arrest all the Jewish children harbored in the village. To his astonishment, the villagers, led by their pastor, refused to obey and sent the police away at immense risk to their own lives.

What was it, Hallie said, about that tiny village in the moun-tains of central France that made him weep? That had wrung the tears from him when all the horrors of the Nazi camps had left him hardened and unmoved? "It was joy that did it, overwhelming joy, which can squeeze tears out of us as suddenly as misery can." His cold, despairing heart, hardened by a thousand tales of un-speakable Nazi brutality, had been burst open by heart-cracking goodness. "I was weeping tears of gratitude. . . . It had to do with the rarity of pure goodness."

WORDS LIKE "GOOD" ARE FOOLISH WORDS

As Hallie read more, he was stunned. Le Chambon had been the safest place for Jews in Nazi-occupied Europe, saving thousands of Jewish children. The pure goodness of the Chambonnais turned Hallie back from suicide that night. But in the weeks that followed he still felt himself torn: his mind was pulled between his old "Cockroach Building" view that life was violent and self-serving, and his new experience of genuine goodness in the world of surrounding evil. Eventually he decided to go to Le Chambon and investigate for himself. When he arrived, he found that Pastor Trocmé, the indomitable Huguenot pastor who had led the Resistance, had died, but his equally indomitable Italian wife, Magda, was still alive. For three hundred years, the Huguenots had themselves been persecuted by the Roman Catholic Church, so on the basis of their faith and their own experience they immediately reached out to shelter the Jewish children—the very children most vulnerable to the hideous Nazi experiments that Hallie had researched. Five thousand endangered Jewish children had been rescued by a few mountain villagers.

Hearing the story recounted in full, Hallie was openly overcome, and found himself muttering to the pastor's wife, "But you are good people, good."

To his amazement, Magda Trocmé responded vehemently. "What did you say? What? Good? *Good*? . . . I'm sorry, but you have not understood what I have been saying. We have been talking about saving the children. We did not do what we did for goodness's sake. We did it for the children. Don't use words like 'good' with me. They are foolish words." The sheer goodness was rare enough, but the goodness was not for the sake of goodness, but for the children.

THE EYE OF THE HURRICANE

Hallie's visit to Le Chambon resolved his doubts about the story as well as his despair in the face of evil, and his book is a magnificent tribute to an easily overlooked aspect of resistance against the Nazis. But when he published his account, he received a dismissive letter from a reader in Massachusetts, arguing that what he had observed was "nothing"—it was inconsequential in terms of the larger historical forces in the war. A little while later, he was lecturing in Minneapolis and a woman with a French accent asked him which Le Chambon it was—there are several French villages by that name.

"Ah," she said, when he told her. "You have been speaking about the village that saved all three of my children." There was utter silence as she went on to thank Hallie for writing the book. Americans were so remote from Europe that they did not understand what the war had meant to ordinary people. "The Holocaust was storm, lightning, thunder, wind, rain, yes. And Le Chambon was the rainbow."

The woman's reference to the ninth chapter of Genesis and to the rainbow as God's guarantee after the flood was like the final piece in the puzzle for Hallie. He knew full well the powerful reality of evil and violence, but its counterbalance was now equally solid. "And yet, and yet—there were Magda and her husband . . . and the villagers of Le Chambon and all those children they had rescued from despair and death." He was beginning to meet more and more of the survivors in New York City, now middle-aged. The villagers had not only saved them, but "had saved their spiritual sanity, their capacity for realistic hope."

Hallie had not only been pulled back from suicide, he had found what he needed and what he was looking for. "Peace sometimes stands like the eye of a hurricane in the very middle of power. The indifferent, destructive power of nature and of fellow-human beings is always near." But the Chambonnais, with their "kitchen-resistance" to murder, had "pushed back the walls of the eye of the hurricane until the murderous winds seemed so far away as to be unreal."

Israel's Yad Vashem medal commemorates those who rescued Jews during the war. A saying from the Talmud is inscribed on it: "Whoever saves a single life is as one who has saved an entire world." The Huguenot villagers had saved five thousand Jewish children; their heart-cracking goodness had also rescued one despairing Jewish professor; and his inspiring account of their story has inspired faith and encouraged hope in countless readers in their turn. Evil, in its unspeakable malignancy, hardens the heart, but there is no heart so hard that goodness and love cannot crack it open.

For Philip Hallie, heart-cracking goodness was the signal of transcendence that punctured his despair and pointed him toward hope. But remember once again that each signal of transcendence sounds out its own special call. No signal is a signal for everyone to hear, so one person's signal is another person's silence. Be ready, then, for the call that comes to you in your life. Whoever has ears to hear, let him hear.

5

STOPPED IN HIS TRACKS
BY A DANDELION

G. K. Chesterton

G. K. Chesterton was a mountain of a man, a Vesuvius of words, with an Everest of a reputation to match. He was larger than life, with a zest for life and fun and a creative imagination that is impossible to describe adequately. He became a famous journalist, author, and debater who was called "the laughing cavalier of Fleet Street," and a "good-humored Kafka." ("He is so gay," Kafka himself said, using the original meaning of the word, "One might almost believe he had found God.") By all accounts, Chesterton was as colorful in person as he was in his writing. From the flourish of his signature to the sweep of his cape, hat, and swordstick, he was a man in whom life and art, reality and imagination had fused happily to create an unforgettable human being.

The author of more than fifty books, the source of countless quotable quotations, the writer of thousands of essays, with even more written about him, Chesterton still defies description. Once when he was speaking, an audience was puzzled when he chuckled aloud while he was saying something serious—only to realize that Chesterton was so far ahead of what he was actually saying that he was laughing at a joke that he was about to make.

Chesterton was born into a comfortable upper-middle-class home in the West End of London. As he grew up, young Gilbert was gifted with a fertile imagination that daily turned the ordinary into the extraordinary and the natural into the magical and mysterious. It was an obvious choice, then, not to go to Oxford and Cambridge along with his best friends from St. Paul's School but to go to art college. In 1892, Chesterton entered the Slade School of Art in London as an eighteen-year-old. "An art school," he wrote after he had become a writer and not the artist he had hoped to be, "is a place where about three people work with feverish energy and everybody else idles to a degree that I should have conceived unattainable by human nature."

Yet art school was where Chesterton, as he put it, "thought my way back to thought itself." The fin-de-siècle climate of late Victorian England was swirling with decadence and cynicism. A form of pessimism that Chesterton called "the black creed" and a "starless nihilism" was all the rage. It left him "on the defensive," and he himself was somewhat drawn to the macabre and the occult. "I dabbled in spiritualism," he wrote later, and he and his brother played with a Ouija board. In his autobiography, he described this period in a chapter titled "How to Be a Lunatic," and he admitted that while his mind was "dreaming and drifting," it was "often drifting onto very dangerous rocks."

One thing held Chesterton back from fully embracing the mood of the times. He was stopped in his tracks by "looking at a dandelion." The world was dark and the world was broken. Cynicism was easy, and anyone could find reasons to be pessimistic about life. But there was more to life than pessimism, and it stood across his path in the form of a common weed, the little yellow-flowered dandelion.

What was life about? Chesterton's friend Hilaire Belloc wrote, "The whole meaning of his life was the discovery, the appreciation of reality." But what did that question mean at the beginning of the twentieth century, and what on earth did a dandelion have to say about reality? For a start, the humble dandelion told Chesterton that there was beauty in the world, and not just brokenness. Both needed to be explained, together. The beauty was as evident as the brokenness, and the brokenness as the beauty. But then, too, there was a wonder in the sheer existence of simple things, such as a dandelion.

What held Chesterton back from a pessimistic view of life, he said later, was a "thin thread of thanks," a sort of "mystical minimum of gratitude." Looking at a humble dandelion, he woke up to wonder and became grateful for life. "I cannot do my duty as a true modern," he wrote, "by cursing everybody who made me whatever I am." Later still, when he wrote as a profession, he confessed, "I was full of a new and fiery resolution to write against the Decadents and the Pessimists who ruled the culture of the age."

Chesterton was not talking about the beauty and the wonder that are so obvious that they are almost a cliché—the miracle of the birth of a baby, the majesty of a sunset over the ocean, or the crystal beauty of a Mozart piano concerto. He was talking of a little common flower that everyone sees, few people pick, and even fewer think about. But thinking about it, he noted that "even mere existence, reduced to its mere primary limits, was extraordinary enough to be exciting." Anything was magnificent compared with nothing. (Leibniz again: "Why is there something and not nothing?")

Gratitude, wonder at the mere existence of simple things—what Chesterton felt about a dandelion, he felt about a daisy too. In a poem he called "The Daisy," he wrote:

> Colossal leagues of powers
> Went to make one daisy.
> And colossal choirs of angels
> Could not give thanks for it.

Sheer beauty, the simple wonder of existence, gratitude for the gift of life—these were G. K. Chesterton's signal of transcendence. He heard the signal loud and clear, and stopped going down the path he was on. But then he had to search. He had to look for a philosophy of life that would allow him to explain both the beauty and the brokenness, which would allow him to be deeply realistic and yet, as he said, to "enjoy enjoyment" and be grateful.

THE REAL DIVISION

Chesterton's story again highlights the point that in the quest for meaning, the important divide is not between believers and unbelievers, or between people of faith and "nones," as it is often put today. The real divide is between those who care enough to ask questions and think seriously about life, and those who are indifferent. And once again, modernity, for all its undoubted blessings, is no help to us at this point. First, it confines us as prisoners in Plato's cave, and then it makes the cave so well-lit, comfortable, and climate-controlled, and provides so many choices and conveniences that sunshine and fresh air hardly seem worth the effort. With so many creature comforts, so many pleasures and entertainments, and the promised metaverse to come, who needs to go out?

Put differently, as modern people we have almost lost our sense
of wonder, and certainly the wonder of existence that inspires the
gratitude to be alive. Thanks to technology and our cities, we
hardly encounter nature at all. Everything in the world around us
is manmade and artificial. Thanks to our "presentism," "genera-
tionalism," and contemporary views of time, we are able to cut off
the only undeniable reminder of our own dependency—our
parents—and thus make the fifth commandment and respect for
parents redundant. And thanks to our political philosophies, we
can banish all sense of indebtedness, dependency, and duty
through invoking the magic word: *rights*. Responsible freedom is
on the way out. Self-reliance, self-discipline, and self-denial are
yesterday's ideals. Duties and demands were for our parents'
world. The result is a generation that is both spoiled and stunted—
spoiled because our psychobabble and our socialist politics have
taught it that the world owes us everything, and stunted because
we have lost our sense of wonder and gratitude to be alive. The
result is simultaneously an inflation of rights and a devaluation
of life.

Humans once encountered nature as power, beauty, and
grandeur—power to be used, beauty to be enjoyed, and grandeur
before which we should stand in awe, and remember our smallness
and the shortness of our lives in contrast to the world around us.
Following the Industrial Revolution, however, nature is over-
whelmingly a power to be used, full stop. The obvious concentration on nature's power is that nature has been exploited to the
point of ruin, and power has been elevated to the level of an idol.
But the other results have been less noticed. We have lessened our
ability to enjoy the beauty of nature, and we have lost our sense
of wonder at the miracle and mystery of human existence and our

own individual existence. Too many modern people live as if society is indebted to them, and they are owed a life—when the fact is that our existence itself is a wonder, and we should ask to whom or to what we owe the response that our lives should be.

EUREKA

It was some years before G. K. Chesterton found the solution to his search, and his description of "the moment of discovery" is an echo of Archimedes's famous cry "Eureka!" as he leaped out of the bath with excitement of his discovery. Wrestling with the polarity of beauty and brokenness, optimism and pessimism, Chesterton was brought up short when he saw that in the Christian view of things both were correct. He recounts his discovery in his book *Orthodoxy*.

> Then I remembered that it was actually the charge against Christianity that it combined these two things that I was wildly trying to combine. Christianity was accused, at one and the same time, of being too optimistic about the universe, and of being too pessimistic about the world. The coincidence made me suddenly stand still.

Chesterton saw, in short, that the Bible's view of creation could explain his optimism and its view of the fall could explain his pessimism, and it brought the two ideas together. His account of his discovery has to be read to be appreciated in all its power and wit, but the key paragraph is clear. The two truths fitted together like a hand in a glove, a key in a lock, or a spike in a hole.

> When once these two parts of two machines had come together, one after another, all the other parts fitted and fell in with an eerie exactitude. I could hear bolt after bolt all over

the machinery falling into its place with a kind of click of relief. Having got one part right, all the other parts were repeating that rectitude, as clock after clock strikes noon. Instinct after instinct was answered by doctrine after doctrine.

The result, Chesterton exulted, allowed him to be both optimistic and pessimistic, and to know where and why each was appropriate. He knew now that the world should have been otherwise, that it was not supposed to be this way, and that it was not his final home. He was therefore able to understand how life had struck him in that odd way, and "why I could feel homesick at home."

Chesterton finished his autobiography just a few weeks before he died. The last chapter he called "The God with the Golden Key," and on the final page he described his faith as "the overwhelming conviction that there is one key which can unlock all doors." The little dandelion had played its humble part in his lifelong engagement with reality.

LET ALL YOUR THINKS BE THANKS

Along with curiosity, question-asking, and wonder, gratitude is increasingly redundant in the world of modernity. We have done it all ourselves, so who is there to thank? Feodor Dostoyevsky could not have been more different. Reprieved by Czar Nicholas I when seconds away from his execution, he never lost his intense sense of wonder and gratitude for being alive. In contrast, he described humanity as the "ungrateful biped."

For Chesterton, gratitude and wonder were simply the fulfillment of how he had begun to think and how he had lived all along. These ideas, he continued, "seem to me to link up my whole life from the beginning, as no other doctrines could do; and especially to settle simultaneously the two problems of my childish happiness and my boyhood brooding." Just before he died, he wrote, "The chief idea of my life," he wrote, is the practice of "taking things with gratitude and not taking things for granted." He passionately agreed with the artist Dante Gabriel Rossetti, "The worst moment for an atheist is when he is genuinely thankful, but has nobody to thank." In his own version, "If my children wake up on Christmas morning and have somebody to thank for putting candy into their stocking, have I no one to thank for putting two feet into mine?" He would certainly have agreed with a line of one of W. H. Auden's last poems, "Let your last thinks all be thanks."

When Chesterton was a young man, a signal of transcendence formed by beauty, wonder, and gratitude punctured the pessimism of his thinking and pointed him toward the giver of such gifts. Do you live in a random universe? Are you merely the product of an accidental encounter of genes seeking to replicate themselves? Or do beauty, wonder, and gratitude speak to you as they did to Chesterton? Each signal of transcendence sounds out its own special call. No signal is a signal for everyone to hear, so one person's signal is another person's silence. Be ready, then, for the call that comes to you in your life. Whoever has ears to hear, let him hear.

6

JOY WITH A CAPITAL J

C. S. Lewis

With around a quarter of a billion of C. S. Lewis's books in print and much-loved films adapted from his novels, Lewis is so well known as a Christian writer and apologist that it is easy to forget that he was once a firmly convinced atheist. Indeed, it was the depth and intensity of his atheism that made him the formidable advocate for the faith that he became. As the profundity of his atheism, so the persuasiveness of his faith. He had known the Christian faith, as he put it, from the outside. His atheism was no casual conviction. He knew it from the inside, he knew many strong atheists, and he had read all the best-known atheist writings from Epicurus and Lucretius to Voltaire, Nietzsche, H. G. Wells, and George Bernard Shaw. And yet his thinking eventually convinced him that atheism did not satisfy.

Lewis described his fifteen-year journey toward faith as an intellectual quest that moved him from atheism and materialism to idealism, to theism, and finally to the Christian faith. Yet his passion for the intellect was balanced by his appreciation of intuition and imagination; throughout the whole quest a recurring signal of transcendence played a key part in turning him around and spurring him on: *Joy*. "All joy wills eternity—wills deep, deep eternity!" Nietzsche's Zarathustra exclaimed in his midnight song. But where Nietzsche did not follow the logic of what he was saying, Lewis did—and it was joy that troubled his atheism and sent him out as a seeker and a "lapsed atheist."

NOTHING BUT DRY HUSKS

C. S. Lewis declared that he was an atheist when he was fourteen years old. From then on, at school in the Malvern Hills in England, throughout the First World War in France, and as a don at Oxford University, he was a self-professedly "good atheist." He was born in Belfast, and his parents were nominally members of the Church of Ireland, but there was no personal faith in the family, and his brother, Warnie, described their parents' faith as the "dry husks of religion." Lewis himself disliked the religion he knew, and described it as a "paralyzing topic."

Several factors combined to drive Lewis to atheism, starting with the death of his mother when he was nine, his father's emotional withdrawal, his extreme unhappiness at school, and later his horrific experiences in the trenches in World War I. This was the period when he loved the music of Richard Wagner, the poems of W. B. Yeats, and the novels of William Morris. After his mother's death, he wrote forlornly, "It was sea and islands now; the great continent had sunk like Atlantis."

Looking back later, Lewis admitted that there was a certain "willful blindness" to his atheism. He disliked all forms of authority, he had a hatred of any outside "interference" in his life, and he found that, contradictorily, he often complained to a God he did not believe in. But above all, it was the autonomy of atheism that appealed to him, along with its view of suffering in the world. With nothing to believe in, there was no one to obey.

In Dostoyevsky's famous words, "everything was permitted." But Lewis, with his active mind, and the dark memory of the Great War to spur him, thought passionately, read voraciously, and debated robustly with his friends. Slowly, over the course of the 1920s he progressed from full-blown materialism to idealism ("all the conveniences of Theism, without believing in God"), then to theism (with the notion of a personal God), and finally—in his brother's sidecar on the way to Whipsnade Zoo—to the Christian faith.

Looking back years later, Lewis was able to trace the hand of God in his journey and described it variously as God's "chess game" against him, God's "fox hunt" with the hounds after him, or the castings of the "Great Angler" who was reeling him in. But viewed from the inside and at the time, nothing was more vital to his rejection of atheism and the intensity of his search than his being "surprised by joy."

MORE TO LIFE THAN MEETS THE MATERIALIST'S EYE

How did joy subvert Lewis's atheism? Years before he met his wife, also named Joy, the idea of joy was so important to Lewis that he called it Joy, with a capital J. In his autobiography, *Surprised by Joy*, Lewis wrote of Joy that in a sense "the central story of my life is about nothing else." At its heart, his life was about longing—"an inconsolable longing"—for something beyond human experience. Such longing was "an unsatisfied desire which is itself more desirable than any other satisfaction." Joy, as he used the word, was sharply distinguished from both pleasure and happiness. Pleasure depends on the five senses—the sight of a beautiful landscape, the taste of a vintage wine, or the smell of an exquisite perfume—and happiness is a matter of circumstances, faring well, and feeling well. Joy, however, transcends both pleasure and happiness. Nietzsche was right: *joy wills eternity*. Or as Lewis described it, "I doubt whether anyone who has ever tasted it would ever, if both were in his power, exchange it for all the pleasures in the world."

Lewis's idea of Joy included beauty, music, poetry, myth, human love, and nature. He tasted Joy as he walked the Mourne Mountains near his home in Northern Ireland, he heard it in the *Ring Cycle* of Richard Wagner, and he encountered it again and again as he read authors such as Spenser, Wordsworth, Coleridge, William Morris, and George MacDonald. One famous moment when Lewis tasted Joy occurred on a summer day when he stood beside a flowering currant bush. Suddenly and without warning the memory rose in him of a time in his old family home in Belfast when his older brother, Warnie, brought his toy garden into the nursery. He was overwhelmed by a sensation of blissful joy. "It was a sensation, of course, of desire; but desire for what? Not, certainly, for a biscuit tin filled with moss, nor even (though that came into it) for my own past—and before I knew what I desired, the desire itself was gone, the whole glimpse withdrawn, the world turned commonplace again, or only stirred by a longing for the longing that had just ceased. It had taken only a moment of time; and in a certain sense everything else that had ever happened to me was insignificant in comparison."

Desire, longing, memory, sensation, a "whiff" of something, "homesickness" for somewhere, "mysterious leaks" of "Something Else" into experience, a world beyond the border of the world, a "Nameless Isle"—Lewis's descriptions of being surprised by Joy are hauntingly evocative. But he always wanted to be precise. The promptings were not nostalgia, a yearning for the past. Nor did they stop and rest on any earthly object. They reach forward and higher and always out of reach—"they are only the scent of a flower we have not found, the echo of a tune we have not heard, news from a country we have never yet visited." Joy was active, and not passive. It beckoned him on. Somehow it seemed to have a mind of its own. The ordinary became extraordinary, but how and why? He had to follow the clues and find the answer.

At first the longing for joy is a rapier-piercing desire for an "unnamable something" triggered by sensations such as the sound of a bell, the smell of a fire, or the sound of birds. But slowly we realize the grail lies beyond all human objects. The Joy was not *in* them; it only came *through* them. Mistake them for the thing itself, and they become "dumb idols." No mountain we can climb, no flower we can find, no horizon we can set out for will ever fulfill our search for joy. If someone follows this quest, Lewis says, "he must come out at last into the clear knowledge that the human soul was made to enjoy some object that is never fully given—in our present mode of subjective and spatio-temporal existence." There was no point in trying to make the Joy last. What mattered was following where the signal pointed. As one biographer wrote, Joy was "almost as a time release capsule that delivers its medicine to the body over a period of time rather than as an injection that delivers the medicine all at once."

A WILL TO JOY?

Ever the serious thinker, Lewis thought long and hard about his experiences of Joy. Were they only a form of Romanticism, on the order of the poet's "heard melodies are sweet, but those unheard are sweeter"? Were they wishful thinking in the manner of Ralph

Waldo Emerson's assertion that "the blazing evidence of immortality is our dissatisfaction with any other solution"? Or was the great Swiss theologian Karl Barth correct—"In every real man the will for life is also the will for joy"? Barth continues, "It is hypocrisy to hide this from oneself. . . . A person who tried to disbar himself from joy is not an obedient person."

Such questions are important, and they must be answered, but the answer lies beyond the experience or the signal itself. As with all signals of transcendence, joy raises questions; it supplies no answers. C. S. Lewis was well trained in Oxford philosophy, and knew too much to leap ahead of the logic of his experience. The signal and its satisfaction were two different things. It was quite possible that reality would never satisfy this unsatisfied desire that was more desirable than any satisfaction. The signal of transcendence punctured the settled assurance of his atheism, and pointed beyond it. But whether there was anything real "beyond," and whether the beyond was solid or insubstantial, he would have to find out for himself—and his search began.

There was one thing about the signal, however, that gave it not only thrust but direction. Lewis pointed out that unless the intimations were capable of fulfillment, the capacity for them is odd. Physical hunger does not prove that someone will find bread—"He may die of starvation on a raft in the Atlantic. But surely a man's hunger does prove that he comes of a race that repairs its body by eating and inhabits a world where eatable substances exist. . . . A man may love a woman and not win her; but it would be very odd if the phenomenon called 'falling in love' occurred in a sexless world." C. S. Lewis, then, became a seeker because of joy just as Malcolm Muggeridge did because of the glimpse of home, W. H. Auden did because of the necessity to judge evil, and

G. K. Chesterton did to justify gratitude. In the lives of each of them there was the major course of the quest still to cover. But the thrust of the questions tore them from their complacency, propelled them across the divide between the indifferent and the concerned, and turned them into seekers.

EGGED ON BY A HARD-BOILED ATHEIST

The broad outlines and the culmination of C. S. Lewis's search are so well known that they need no repeating. But curiously one of the key moments in his search was triggered by "the hardest boiled of all the atheists I knew." He had finished reading G. K. Chesterton's *The Everlasting Man* when T. D. Weldon, a fellow don at Magdalen College, sat by his fire and remarked that the evidence for the historicity of the Gospels was "surprisingly good." "Rum thing," Weldon said, "all that stuff of Frazer's [*The Golden Bough*] about the Dying God. Rum thing. It almost looks as if it had really happened once."

Weldon's remark was shattering to Lewis. "If he, the cynic of cynics, the toughest of the toughs, were not—as I would still have put it—'safe,' where could I turn? Was there then no escape?" Lewis turned to study the Gospels, became convinced of their truth, and not too long after reached the moment he described so memorably:

> You must picture me alone in that room in Magdalen, night after night, feeling, whenever my mind lifted even for a second from my work, the steady, unrelenting approach of Him who I desired so earnestly not to meet. That which I greatly feared had at last come upon me. In the Trinity Term of 1929 [actually 1930] I gave in, and admitted that God

was God, and knelt and prayed: perhaps, that night, the most dejected and reluctant convert in all England.

FORGET THE SIGNALS

Being "surprised by joy" was all important to C. S. Lewis, but he was clear that the signals and signposts were only signs, and they could be forgotten in the full satisfaction of the discovery they pointed to. Such signals are invaluable today in prompting people to think and search, especially those who think more deeply. At the very least, the signals hint loudly that there is far more to reality than the world experienced through the five senses, the prison world of Plato's cave. For those who hear the signals and pay attention, they compel them to see that "reality is very odd, and that the ultimate truth, whatever it may be, *must* have the characteristics of strangeness."

At the same time, Lewis warned, there was a danger in idolizing such experiences in themselves and therefore of failing to go beyond them. Those who make that mistake have stopped too soon. They have reached only "the suburbs of Jerusalem" and the "outskirts of heaven," but they have yet to reach the city itself. Too much gazing at the moon may make someone a lunatic, he said, but it is an equal mistake to forget that the beauty of the moon is only "sunlight at second hand," so we would be wise to press on to see the sun itself.

Lasting pleasure and true happiness are rare enough, but Joy is at another level altogether, so the signal of transcendence that points to such joy will be almost irresistible. But remember once again that each signal of transcendence sounds out its own special call. No signal is a signal for everyone to hear, so one person's signal is another person's silence. Be ready, then, for the call that comes to you in your life. Whoever has ears to hear, let him hear.

7

THE HAUNTING
CARICATURE

Windsor Elliott

Supermodels seem to be everywhere these days, as the term has been inflated and used indiscriminately. But in the late sixties they were a rare breed whose faces and names were recognized internationally. Many of those most famous names—Jean Shrimpton, Veruschka, Twiggy, Lauren Hutton—are still known today because of their enduring work. But one name, known among the highest-paid photographic fashion models at the time, is not so well known today because she left the fashion world at the height of her career—just as her fourth *Vogue* cover was hitting the newsstands. She left abruptly because a signal of transcendence stopped her in her tracks and sent her in an entirely different direction.

Windsor Elliott, as she was known in the fashion world, was not the name her parents gave her when she was born in Southern California. She chose it on a whim as a temporary professional name for a series of fashion shoots in a summer job in San Francisco. She had driven up from Los Angeles in her fire-engine-red Stingray, bringing along a book by Jean Shrimpton, the English fashion cover-girl icon and girlfriend of Mick Jagger, and thought, *Why not fashion modeling for a summer job?* She imagined it would be only a brief and fun adventure during her summer vacation from the University of Southern California. But to her surprise, the summer work exploded into a career too lucrative to abandon. Instead, she postponed returning to her studies and found herself launching out from San Francisco to Toronto, then to Paris, and finally to New York.

In New York, Windsor became a "Ford model," working for the legendary Eileen Ford, who had begun with two telephones in the 1940s and built her agency into a billion-dollar international business that was the most famous in the world. By the late sixties, when Windsor arrived in New York, the fashion world was at the height of its creativity, glamour, and power. Diana Vreeland, the editor-in-chief of *Vogue* magazine, was the reigning empress of the limitless imagination for the fashion industry ("Fake it, Fake it, Fake it!"). Photographers such as Richard Avedon, Irving Penn, and Patrick Lichfield created the iconic images and conjured the "must have" looks that shaped the tastes of the international jet set and led much of popular culture worldwide.

For Windsor as a new arrival, daily life in New York was a breathless round of cab rides to auditions, fittings, photo shoots, dinners, parties, and events. From Clairol to Clinique, from Bergdorf's to Bonwit's, from A to Z—Chanel to Yves Saint-Laurent—her face began appearing on page after page and product after product. Her apartment was a beautiful turn-of-the-century, historic restoration on the Upper East Side, close to Central Park. Her favorite place to regroup was in front of the vast marble fireplace in the quiet of her apartment with its soaring ceilings and French doors to the sunlit balcony. The world, it seemed, was her oyster.

Windsor's first *Vogue* cover was shot by a young French photographer of her own age. Baron Arnaud de Rosnay was a tall, handsome, elegant aristocrat, whose family's high lineage even possessed the ancient right to ride into Notre Dame cathedral on a horse. Almost immediately they became an inseparable pair, and soon Windsor was wearing Arnaud's ring—"a match made in Condé Nast heaven," as the formidable Diana Vreeland pronounced it. For Windsor and Arnaud that meant location shoots and crisscrossing the Atlantic for them to spend time together. They had extraordinary adventures, but it was their shared questions about life—deep and serious questions in both their hearts—that meant the most to Windsor.

UNFORGOTTEN QUESTIONS

Windsor definitely had searching questions, and below the gloss and glamour of her career she was always thinking, thinking, thinking. Her parents had divorced when she was four. Each of them then had partners who were alcoholics and, in both cases, violent. When her mother's boyfriend committed suicide, her mother slid into an emotional meltdown, and the toll on the divided family was disastrous. It led to a bitter custody battle between her parents. With neither side willing to compromise, the judge made Windsor a ward of the State of California, and she was taken into "protective care."

The juvenile center, McLaren Hall in Los Angeles, was a Dickensian warehouse for children. It was later the subject of a book and a Hollywood film *White Oleander*, and has since been the subject of documentaries, class-action suits, and finally, in response to wide condemnation, demolished. It was a Bentham-like panopticon of surveillance where the children were watched continuously, including all night long, in windowless locked cells and subjected to a harsh authoritarian regime. Within days of being placed there, Windsor's father's lawyer secured her release. But for Windsor, this experience of the social horror of children in supposed "protective care" was a nightmare of brutality and injustice that left her with questions forever pressing for answers. She requested of her parents, and they agreed to her boarding the final two years of high school at Westlake School for Girls in Bel Air, which allowed her to put much of the darkness and chaos behind her. To that point they were the happiest and most life-giving days of her life.

The early experiences were indelible, however, and they were later compounded by the specter of the Vietnam War. Windsor's stepbrother, almost her own age, was killed in Vietnam and many of her school and college peers had been drafted to join the senseless carnage in the jungles and paddy fields of Asia.

There was no real faith in Windsor's family. Her father had been turned off by the legalism of his own parents. Mention of religion at the dining table would bring a plate banged down on the table to end the conversation. Her mother, like many in California, was interested in everything New Age, and for a while she followed Guru Paramahansa Yogananda. He was the first Indian guru to settle permanently in the United States, and his work would later be promoted by Steve Jobs, the genius behind Apple. For her part, Windsor ignored the paths her parents took and was only too eager to make her own way in life. Religion played no part in her sense of freedom and self-reliance that New York and the fashion world offered.

SALVADOR DALÍ'S CHEETAH

The weekend that changed Windsor's life forever began like many others. She and Arnaud often spent glorious, carefree weekends in the French capital, usually attending dinner parties hosted by Arnaud's illustrious friends. Among them were such notable figures as the Duke and Duchess of Windsor, the Rothschilds, the von Fürstenbergs, and artists such as Pablo Picasso and Salvador Dalí. On this particular weekend, Dalí and his wife and muse, Gala, hosted a party in their stunning apartments in the Hotel Meurice, opposite the Tuileries Garden.

Spectacular evenings at the time brought out the most extravagantly dressed guests and reflected the sweeping fascination with India just ignited by the Beatles' odyssey to the Maharishi's ashram in Rishikesh. Gold-encrusted Nehru jackets were the rage for the men, while the women glided swanlike in gold-embroidered caftans with jeweled turbans in their hair. The parties Dalí gave reached a level of opulence and extravagance that was unmatched in their time. And of course, Dalí himself was ground zero for surrealism in the sixties—in his life, not just in his art.

As gorgeous as the other guests were, what stunned Windsor was not the people, but a breathtakingly beautiful jungle animal pacing among the guests. It was Dalí's pet cheetah, "Babou." The little cheetah, as it was called, was actually an ocelot, or dwarf leopard, which was an endangered species from South America and had supposedly been given to Dalí by a head of state. For a while it accompanied him everywhere, with its stone-studded collar and jeweled leash. According to one account, Dalí once took the wild cat to a Manhattan restaurant and tethered it to the table, causing considerable alarm to a fellow diner. To calm the lady's fears, he blithely assured her that Babou was actually an enormous domestic cat that he had "painted over in an op art design."

The night of Dalí's party in the Meurice, Windsor watched the cheetah with fascination. Secured to an ornate table in the middle of the room by a long and elegant leash, it was pacing among some of the most legendary personalities in Europe. Beautiful, lithe, imperious but now domesticated, the stunning creature had been apparently declawed and presumably de-everything-elsed. In a single instant Windsor felt hit by an inexplicable sadness that this magnificent creature had been reduced to a caricature of the animal it was born to be. And then, as Windsor's eye traveled the room to all the illustrious guests with their stunning costumes, she was struck again with the thought: these are the beautiful people . . . they fill the fashion pages and the social columns . . . this is what the rest of the world admires and aspires to . . . yet somehow there is something about all this that is making a caricature of us too. She felt she was suddenly looking into an abyss of absurdity and meaninglessness. The sparkling party had stopped for a second in suspended animation and something very deep and hollow was exposed.

At what was arguably the ground zero of surrealism, a little cheetah pacing among golden caftans and titled heads had opened up a huge incongruity. These were "The Beautiful People" (as the *Vogue* column called them), some of them extraordinarily gifted and many of them truly wonderful. But what Windsor felt they were swept up in was not.

Desmond Morris had written a bestseller, *The Naked Ape*, but as many have pointed out, the reality is quite the opposite. Humans are the one form of life on earth that does not stay naked.

They wear clothes, entirely artificial coverings. And the wilder, the more artificial, and the more expensive the clothes, the deeper and more complex the motives behind them and the statements they are designed to make.

TILL WE HAVE FACES

Returning to New York, Windsor made an inner commitment to begin a search for the real meaning of life and, with her lifetime of questions, whether there was a God. Not knowing where to begin, she followed the suggestions of editors at *Vogue* and found herself traveling down strange, mystical, and sometimes occult paths, only to find dead end after dead end. On the question of evil, she was urged to see that the evil she encountered at McLaren Hall was only part of what the Eastern religions call *maya*, or illusion. But she felt that kind of worldview gave her no answer or foundation for the justice she wanted for the innocent children trapped there. Finally, close to giving up, as she walked up Park Avenue one summer evening, she cried out in the darkness, "God, I can't find you. If you are there, will you please find me?"

Windsor has written the story of her life in her memoir, *Faces*. It includes the account of her search and how it ended. The title by itself tells the story of one of her key themes. In her field of fashion photography, the unique asset each person has is obviously their face, but she was intrigued to realize that there is more to our "faces" than we often think. In fact, there are really three faces we each have—the face we are born with, the faces we learn to put on throughout our lives—whether cosmetically or socially—and the face we are becoming through the choices that form our inner character.

Usually, we only think of the first two faces, and how we can conceal the flaws of the first with products and procedures that promise to recreate the second. But the more important gap is not between the first and second faces but between the second and third. Windsor saw that it is what one is *becoming*—the growth or the degeneration in character—that is the deeper meaning of what begins to show in the face. George Orwell once remarked of someone, "He wears a mask, and his face grows to fit it." As Windsor explores in her book, that third meaning of face lay behind Oscar Wilde's haunting novel *The Picture of Dorian Gray*, and it lies behind C. S. Lewis's own favorite of all his many books, *Till We Have Faces*. Windsor wishes she could have borrowed it as the title of her own book; she believes it says it all.

"Absurdity," "caricature," "incongruity," "discrepancy"—each is a single, simple word, but together they join hands to point toward a chasm laid bare when any veneer of unreality is removed—whether slowly eroded or suddenly torn off—to reveal a deeper reality of emptiness where meaning is longed for. Where did that irresistible sense of *caricature* come from? Where did the sense of incongruity between who we know we are and what we somehow know we were meant to be come from? The quiet discrepancy between what we know in our heart of hearts is true and what we know is false? At least that insistent discrepancy sheds the ill-fitting pretense that this is all there is—and signals that there has to be more, so the search for a better answer and a deeper meaning is given its burning agenda.

As Windsor's story shows, signals of transcendence can come in an instant and out of nowhere. And as Peter Berger points out, there are other signals of transcendence that are also triggered by a similar sense of the incongruous—for example, humor. A situation can suddenly become funny when two entirely independent events can be interpreted in two entirely different ways at the same time. Often, it is the punch line, the unexpected denouement, or the pratfall that reveals a new and quite different meaning.

✺

Berger points out that both comedy and tragedy turn on the same vast discrepancy between a human and the universe he finds himself in, but they lead in entirely different directions. In tragedy, there is nothing anyone can do. The outcome is inescapable fate—for Oedipus or Hamlet, for example—and the only appropriate response of the audience is pity at the sight of the inescapable suffering. But in comedy, if only briefly, the outcome is an escape from the seemingly fixed and determined, and a release from the inevitable, which lifts the spirit and inspires hope. From the comic perspective, the world is not ironclad after all. The jack-in-the-box springs out again. There is another way of seeing things, and a glimmer of possibility is opened.

One of the most extraordinary experiences of my life was meeting an old Jewish gentleman in Poland who had survived Auschwitz. His very faith in God, he said, had been saved from despair by a fellow believer whose sense of humor was irrepressible, whatever they faced. There was nothing at all humorous about their suffering, and they never made light of the evil and the horror, but even when they were yards from the gas ovens, humor meant that heaven relativized the earth, and hope transcended and relativized even Hitler.

Needless to say, the signal of transcendence is once again only a signal. It is a pointer, and not a proof, so the searcher must search and only a warranted faith can provide an answer that is solid and not a mirage. What did the signal point to? Did Windsor's sense of yawning absurdity suggest that all that lies below the supposed reality of the everyday world is *maya*, or illusion, as the Hindus believe? Or is there grounding for a richer and more solid reality behind our world that undergirds and gives meaning to the reality of this world? Readers of Windsor's memoir can see how she finds that the latter, not the former, is the answer.

For Windsor Elliott, the signal of transcendence punctured her world of glamour and success. It pointed her toward a deeper reality and meaning beyond the artificial and the ever-changing. But remember again that each signal of transcendence sounds out its own special call. No signal is a signal for everyone to hear, so one person's signal is another person's silence. Be ready, then, for the call that comes to you in your own life. Whoever has ears to hear, let him hear.

8

THE TRUTH
WE FACE ALONE

Leo Tolstoy

F ew great men have inspired so many others, and have simultaneously been despised by so many others, as Leo Tolstoy. Different people took different sides over different periods of his life—about which he himself had passionately different views at different times. Along with Alexander Pushkin and Feodor Dostoyevsky, Tolstoy is one of the three giants of nineteenth-century Russian literature, a master of realistic fiction, and one of the greatest novelists of all time. Poet and critic Matthew Arnold declared that a novel by Tolstoy was not a work of art, but a piece of life. Many thought that Tolstoy had almost godlike powers. People who visited him in his old age sometimes felt uncomfortable in his presence because he appeared to understand their unspoken thoughts.

If Tolstoy's life had stopped when he was in his forties, his legacy would have been clear and indisputable. He was the universally acclaimed author of *War and Peace* and *Anna Karenina*, two of the very greatest novels ever written, and he was hailed as a literary genius on a par with Dante and Shakespeare. The trouble was not that Tolstoy then went in a different direction and was unable to take his readers with him. It was that he himself was profoundly dissatisfied with the direction he had taken up to that point, so he struck out in a radically new direction, to the dismay of many who loved and admired him, including his wife and a large number of his family, his friends, and his readers.

At the end of Tolstoy's life, he was nominated several times for both the Nobel Peace Prize and the Nobel Prize for Literature, but each time he was passed over. The controversy continues to this day. That one of the most illustrious writers in all history was turned down for the literature prize is unfathomable, but it shows how controversial Tolstoy had become. He wrote his first two masterpieces after he returned from fighting in the Crimean War. Until then, he says, he had lived a lax and promiscuous life that was typical of the privileged class of his time in Russia. His philosophy was to fall in line with the thinking around him ("like a person in a boat carried along by the wind and the waves")—at the University of Kazan, as a wealthy young aristocrat living off his vast estate, as a returning officer, and as a traveler on his two trips to Europe.

In his forties, however, Tolstoy experienced a deep and sudden crisis, and by the time he was fifty-one, he struck out in the new direction that he describes in his memoir *Confession*. No more the master of realist fiction, he poured out a series of moral and religious stories. Ashamed of his partying, gambling, whoring younger self, he became the prophetic and proselytizing Christian anarchist and humanist, who was seen by some as "the conscience of the world." His ideals of pacifism and nonviolence directly influenced both Mahatma Gandhi, who corresponded with him, and Martin Luther King Jr. He also spurred the rise of many

"Tolstoyan communities" across the world, as well as some famous experiments in democratic education.

Tolstoy's wife, Sonya, had borne him thirteen children, and she had also been his secretary, editor, and manager, who took down the great works he dictated. She and his family were therefore greatly dismayed when he renounced his title as count, announced that he would live from then on as plain Leo Nikolayevich, and publicly declared that all his post-1880s writings were public property. Looking back, he referred to his novel *Anna Karenina* as "an abomination that no longer exists for me."

IS THERE MEANING IN LIFE THAT DEATH DOES NOT DESTROY?

What happened to Tolstoy? Pouring back over the evidence of his earlier life, many have searched for the clues that led to his great crisis and his radical transformation. There is no question that his yearning for truth, his search for the meaning of life, and his interest in religious questions had been threads running through all his life, but they intensified with the writing of *Anna Karenina*, which he found difficult to complete. "Today," his wife wrote at the time, "he says he cannot live for long in this terrible religious struggle." It was just after that time that he read Pascal's *Pensées* and began a spiritual and intellectual retreat in order to think things over and resolve the momentous conflict in his mind.

The crisis had nothing to do with Tolstoy's circumstances. He wrote that he had started to think more deeply at a time when he was surrounded by, as he stated,

> complete happiness. I was not yet fifty, I had a kind, loving and beloved wife, lovely children, and a large estate that

was growing and expanding with no effort on my part. I was respected by relatives and friends far more than ever before. I was praised by strangers and could consider myself a celebrity without deceiving myself. Moreover I was not unhealthy in mind or body, but on the contrary enjoyed a strength of mind and body as I had rarely witnessed in my contemporaries.

In short, Tolstoy could not have asked for more from his life. So what happened? A signal of transcendence sounded loudly at the very center of Tolstoy's thinking—death, his own death, and the challenge of what his life and work meant in light of his coming death. He was healthy and strong enough, he said, to outlast the peasants working in the fields, but death haunted him.

Today or tomorrow sickness will come (and they had already arrived) to those dear to me, and to myself, and nothing will remain. . . . Sooner or later my deeds, whatever they may have been, will be forgotten and will no longer exist. . . . It is only possible to go on living while you are intoxicated with life; once sober, it is impossible not to see that it is all a mere trick, and a stupid trick!

Tolstoy recounted "an old Eastern fable"—a story that I often heard growing up in China. A traveler, suddenly confronted by a ferocious wild animal, took refuge in an empty well, only to discover that at the bottom was a dragon waiting to devour him. Grabbing a branch as he fell, he hung on, with the snarling animal above him and the open jaws of the dragon below him. But then to his horror, he saw two mice, one white and one black, steadily gnawing at the branch on which he was hanging.

His only relief was some drops of honey on the leaves of the bush, which he licked as he waited for his inevitable fall and his end. He wrote,

> In the same way, I am clinging to the tree of life, knowing full well that the dragon of death inevitably awaits me, ready to tear me to pieces, and I cannot understand how I have fallen into this torment. And I try licking the honey that once consoled me [which he says later were his two loves, for his family and for his writing], but it no longer gives me pleasure. . . . I can see the dragon clearly and the honey no longer tastes sweet. I can see only one thing; the inescapable dragon and the mice, and I cannot tear my eyes away from them. And this is no fable but the truth, the truth that is irrefutable and intelligible to everyone.

This brief summary may make Tolstoy's crisis sound purely emotional, but if that is so, the brevity is misleading. He recounts the twists and turns of his thinking through the philosophies of his day, and his "moments of bewilderment" that raised question after question for any firm conclusion he thought he had reached. Always the questions kept coming, *Why this? Why that? And then what?* "And I had absolutely no answer. . . . My life came to a standstill. . . . The truth was that life is meaningless." He then thought of his family. "If I love them, I cannot conceal the truth from them. Each step taken in knowledge leads them to this truth. And the truth is death."

For Tolstoy, there was no answer to be found in science and the "rational knowledge" of the nineteenth century. The brilliance of science lies in its capacity to answer the *how* questions, but it has nothing to say about *why*. After his careful consideration of all he had been taught and all he had encountered, he concluded wryly: "It is now clear to me that there was no difference between our behavior and that of people in a madhouse; but at the time I only dimly suspected this and, like all madmen, I thought everyone was mad except myself." He concluded that rationalism was a dead end, and the central dilemma of his life was meaninglessness of life in the face of death. Death had thrown down a gauntlet and forced him to weigh the meaning of his life from the perspective of the certainty of his death.

I searched all branches of knowledge and not only found nothing, but was convinced that all those who had searched the realms of knowledge like myself had likewise found nothing. Not only had they found nothing, but they plainly acknowledged the same thing that had led me to despair: the meaninglessness of life as the only indisputable piece of knowledge available to man.

His conclusion was blunt.

My question, the one that brought me to the point of suicide when I was fifty years old, was a simple one that lies in the soul of every person, from a silly child to a wise old man. It is the question without which life is impossible, as I had learned from experience. It is this: what will come of what I do today or tomorrow? What will come of my entire life? Expressed another way, the question can be put like this: why do I live? Why do I wish for anything, or do anything? Or expressed another way: is there any meaning in my life that will not be annihilated by the inevitability of death which awaits me?

Tolstoy expressed the same point unforgettably in the mouth of Ivan, the leading character in his novella *The Death of Ivan Ilyich*, "What if my whole life has been wrong?"

Tolstoy set out his rigorous thinking and the development of his intellectual and spiritual journey in his memoir *Confession*. "Failing to find an explanation in knowledge, I began to search for it in life." All that lay behind his crisis and the eventual direction his search took need not concern us here, but there is no doubt that the spur was the centrality of death. He emphatically rejected Russian Orthodoxy and was excommunicated in his turn, and he was also roundly attacked by Lenin for the effects of his pacifism in hampering the revolution of 1905. In the end, Tolstoy put his trust in the simple faith of the Russian peasants and in his own carefully tailored version of Jesus.

Some have found Tolstoy's *Gospel in Brief*, his harmony of the four Gospels, to be inspiring. Philosopher Ludwig Wittgenstein carried it around with him in the First World War. "This book virtually kept me alive," he said. Many others find it entirely unsatisfactory. Like Thomas Jefferson before him, Tolstoy had taken the story of Jesus and shorn off everything miraculous and supernatural, and it was this watered-down gospel that made his final years so controversial. He offended those who disliked religion of any kind, and he equally offended those who championed a more orthodox faith. In the place of a Russian Orthodox cross, he wore a medallion around his neck with a portrait of Jean Jacques Rousseau. But what is indisputable throughout all these controversies is the signal of transcendence that triggered his search and change of heart—his own mortality.

I AM I, AND I WON'T BE HERE FOREVER

Tolstoy's brush with death was strong—some would say extreme. But in fact our own death is a truth that each of us must face alone, a truth each of us must take seriously if we are to lead an examined life. If you think about it, there are two moments in each of our lives that are critical for us all, yet often barely noticed at the time. The first is when we come to realize, and say to ourselves in effect, "I am I." We enter life from our mother's womb, and most also grow up in the heart of a family that loves us; only slowly do we become aware of our own individuality. We are not our parents, and we are not our brothers and sisters. We are each ourselves, individual and unique. If this sense of growing individuality is overdeveloped, we may become narcissists ("I am, and who but I?"), but if it is underdeveloped, we may suffer from separation anxiety and develop a fear of living so that we, too, easily become dependent.

The second crucial moment is when we realize, either faintly or loudly, "I am I, and I won't be here forever." In other words, we realize our own mortality. The day is coming when we won't be here, when almost no one will know we have been here, and life will go on as if we have never been here. For almost all of us, in short, there will be no trace of us left on the earth. If this sense is overdeveloped, it may lead to a fear of death that can paralyze—as it did Tolstoy for a while. But equally, if it is underdeveloped, it may lead to a blithe denial of death that promotes a view of life as a grand "immortality project"—as if we, or our fame and legacy, could live forever if only we succeed in stamping our achievements on history.

In sum, life is short and death is certain, so what does that mean for how we see life? For the Greeks, it meant that humans, for all our greatness, are always "mortals." For the Romans, it meant a simple epitaph, "As I, so you, so everyone." What, then, does our life add up to in light of the final factor of death? How do we live well and live wisely?

Thinking through life in the face of death is both bracing and more common than many might realize. There is of course one major world religion that started that way. The privileged young Nepali prince Siddhartha Gautama, who was to become the Buddha, started exactly like that. Growing up insulated from real life, he was said to have been jolted into searching by a chariot ride on which he encountered an old man, a sick man, and a dead man. Those incidents set him off on the long path that led him to Varanasi and to his claim to enlightenment sitting under the Bodhi tree.

Tolstoy's great contemporary Feodor Dostoyevsky was another who was shaped by an unforgettable brush with death. In April 1849, in his twenties, he was arrested as a member of the Petrashevsky circle, accused of antigovernment activities, and imprisoned for a year in the Peter and Paul Fortress in St. Petersburg. He was condemned to execution by firing squad; ordered to kneel in the square, he was then blindfolded and tied to a pillar. He heard the roll of the drums, but seconds before what he believed was his death, he was reprieved by Czar Nicholas I. The mock execution was intended not as an act of mercy, but as psychological terror. It shaped Dostoyevsky's gratitude for life forever and resulted eventually in a Christian faith that was both deeper and more orthodox than Tolstoy's. His was a faith, he said in his last notebook, that was not naive and untested "like some schoolboy; but my hosanna has passed through a great furnace of doubt."

Quite different, but equally extraordinary, was the experience of Alfred Nobel, the Swedish inventor and business leader now celebrated as the donor of the Nobel Prizes—given to those who, "during the preceding year, shall have conferred the greatest benefit on mankind." Nobel was an unlikely person to present a Nobel Peace Prize, as he and his family were associated with war, not peace. In 1867, he had invented dynamite, which was widely used in both construction and warfare. He owned more than three hundred patents for detonators, and he also owned more than one hundred factories that made explosives and other weapons.

Nobel never said what was behind his late-life decision to devote his fortune to charity, so the reason is not clear. But many believe it was spurred by an extraordinary case of mistaken identity. While in South Africa in 1888, on opening the morning newspaper, Nobel was startled to read his own obituary. In fact, it was his older brother Ludwig who had died of a heart attack in Cannes, but what he read was the headline, "The merchant of death is dead," followed by a scathing obituary. "Dr. Alfred Nobel, who became rich by finding more ways to kill people faster than ever before, died yesterday." The error was quickly corrected, but the damage was done. If the account is true, Nobel had the unusual experience of reading what people really thought of him. It pained him so much that he became obsessed with his posthumous reputation. He was fortunate to have another ten years of life after that, during which he amended his plans, changed his will, and rearranged his bequests. More than 90 percent of his wealth went to the Nobel Prizes. It was, as one biographer said, "a cause upon which no future obituary writer would be able to cast aspersions."

The signal of transcendence sounded powerfully in all these cases, though the responses were very different. Alberto Giacometti, the Swiss sculptor and close friend of Pablo Picasso, described the effect of death as a "hole torn in life." In his case, he was shocked to his core by the death of a close friend when he was nineteen. The questions that death raised gripped him for more than a quarter of a century and shaped him as the artist of the fragile, the alienated, and the impermanent.

For Leo Tolstoy, death as a signal of transcendence punctured the world of his privilege, wealth, success, and fame, and pointed him toward the faith that gave his life meaning. There is no more powerful and universal signal than death, but even death can be denied until it comes. Remember, then, that each signal of transcendence sounds out its own special call. No signal is a signal for everyone to hear, so one person's signal is another person's silence. Be ready for the call that comes to you in your own life. Whoever has ears to hear, let him hear.

9

IF LOVE IS
NOT FOREVER

Whitfield Guinness

I never knew my Irish grandfather Whitfield, my father's father. He died in China nearly a hundred years ago when my father was a teenager at school in England. But I grew to know him through my Swedish grandmother Jane, who lived for about forty years after my grandfather's untimely death. She was an extraordinary presence in our lives. Tall, regal, commanding, and beautiful even in old age, my grandfather called her "Queenie" because of her beauty and her bearing. Her life of ninety-nine years spanned the Victorian age to the 1960s, and from the Swedish court to imperial China and the war-ravaged countryside of provincial life under the Manchus, and then back to southern Sweden. Often, she would tell stories from her rich memories, and then she would smile sweetly and say in her lilting Swedish accent, "I only wish you had known your grandfather."

Whitfield and Jane met in China. Jane had been to a finishing school in Paris and had been brought up in aristocratic circles in Stockholm. She was a close friend of Prince Oscar Bernadotte and the royal family. It was a considerable shock to her family and friends when she announced that she was going to China as a missionary. It must have been an equal shock to her when she discovered on arrival that China was convulsing with the rebellion of the Boxers, or "the Society of the Righteous Fists."

Whitfield Guinness was a young Irish doctor who came to China in his twenties. He had been born in Paris just before the Franco-Prussian war, was educated at Gonville and Caius College at Cambridge, and trained at the London Hospital. When he arrived in Henan Province, and his senior colleague went home on furlough, he found himself the only doctor in a province the size of Britain, with no nurses and no other medical personnel. His first case made him a celebrity. A tailor had swallowed a needle and was brought to him half dead after the local medicine men had failed to help the poor man. His remedy was hailed as a miracle, as was the fact that he charged nothing. Working to found and build a hospital in the ancient imperial capital of Kaifeng, his medical exploits over the next decades were prodigious. When he died of typhoid after treating an imperial soldier, he left what is today a flourishing military hospital.

It was the Boxer Rebellion in 1900 that brought my grandparents together. Antiforeign sentiment was running high in the late nineteenth century, and a month before the rebellion, the flinty old Empress Dowager had issued a decree, "Foreigners must be killed! Even if they retire, foreigners are still to be killed." By the time the rebellion was over, 250 missionaries and 32,000 "secondary devils" (Chinese Christians) had been slaughtered. Westerners were hacked to death, children were beheaded in front of their parents' eyes, and carts were driven backward and forward over the bodies of young Chinese women until they were dead.

My grandfather's escape became legendary. Still in his twenties and only recently arrived in China, he found himself in charge of a small group of Westerners that included a six-week-old baby. A thousand miles of Boxer-infested country lay between them in Henan and the safety of the coast. Overland travel was out of the question, and because of drought, the one waterway was not navigable. Defenseless, they sought shelter with a neighbor whose son's life they had saved. Behind them, their premises were ransacked, looted, and burned to the ground; knowing the superstition of the Chinese they decided to hide in a derelict haunted attic. "Were they afraid?" their host asked. "Afraid?" Whitfield replied. "That's the very thing. The more haunted the better!" They huddled there in filth and sweltering hundred-degree heat for five days with only a little Chinese tea and some bread, but no water or bathroom. The rampaging mob swarmed all around them, hammering on the roof and threatening to burn the building down to see if they were there. But not once did the baby cry and they were not discovered.

The sixth day of the riot was the worst. The conditions had become unimaginable, and they were exhausted. The women were sick, and one of the men thought he was done for. Only Whitfield was still well, and capable of leading and encouraging them. At one point, as he sat cross-legged on the trapdoor that guarded their hiding place, a sword or bayonet came right up between his legs. He felt the trapdoor move slightly underneath him as the rioter pressed it upward, but he pressed back down on it with all his might. "Quite unmovable!" a voice shouted in Mandarin, and the voices died away as the noisy mob swarmed away to search elsewhere. In the near darkness, he wrote what he believed would be his last words addressed to his father in London—a page in the family Bible that we still possess and cherish.

Eventually, Whitfield helped the tiny band to slip away under cover of darkness and a torrential downpour that made the river navigable again. They then found a boat and, in disguise, made their way down the Yellow River on a perilous, two-week journey to Hankow and to safety. Thirty days after the rebellion broke out, and still constantly on the alert, they rounded a bend in the river; to their indescribable relief, they saw foreign warships moored in the harbor. When the bedraggled little group showed up at the home of friends, one journal commented, "Received from the dead." Unbeknown to the little group that had huddled in the haunted attic, thirty-seven colleagues and their children had been slaughtered in the capital of the province next to them on that opening day of the rebellion. With no news of them for a month, their colleagues in the coastal cities feared that they had been slaughtered too.

The silver lining in the Boxer Rebellion for Whitfield Guinness was his meeting and marrying Jane af Sandberg, the beautiful young Swedish missionary who had been forced to leave the city she was in and come to the safety of Shanghai—where they met and married. Although many had died, they had both been spared, and Whitfield more dramatically. But after such a lengthy nightmare and such a close brush with death, life could never be the same for either of them. Over a long, dangerous month Whitfield had been an inch from death every day. He had lost everything—his clothes, books, medical instruments, and all the personal belongings that he had brought to China. But he had survived, whereas many of his friends and colleagues had lost their lives and their families.

From that day on, Whitfield and Jane's gratitude and their love for each other had an intensity fired in the crucible in which they had lived and continued to live. On my desk in front of me as I write is a little love note Whitfield wrote to Jane on their first Christmas Day together: *"To One who is dearer than life: With a love that is stronger than death."* Dearer than life, stronger than death. Was this wording his own, or was he quoting someone else's tribute? I don't know. But what is plain is that their love in the face of death signaled a love that is stronger than death, and that pointed beyond this life to a greater reality that would have to be true if such a cry was to be satisfied and such a passionate love was to be fulfilled.

THE ULTIMATE SIGNAL

The glory of love is a human overflowing with life. Love is so exuberant with life and joy and beauty and hope that it desires to burst out of the very bounds of time and become timeless. Love wills eternity. Love is the ultimate signal of transcendence. As Roberta Flack sang in her song, "The First Time Ever I Saw Your Face," "I knew our joy would fill the earth / and last 'til the end of time."

Unlike the other people in these stories, neither Whitfield nor Jane needed prompting to be seekers. They were already believers, and it was their faith that sent them to China to serve the Chinese people. But the signal still sounds out clearly. Their love for each other, the love they experienced and expressed in the face of death, was as powerful a signal of transcendence as any of the other stories we have shared.

The unknown poet singer of the Song of Songs declared famously, "Love is as strong as death" (Song of Songs 8:6). Those who experience love in the face of death go further: Love is stronger than death. Love will flout family feuds, as Romeo and Juliet did for the Montagues and Capulets. Love will climb every mountain, cross every valley, and even swim the Hellespont by night, as Leander did for Hero. Fire cannot destroy love. Waters cannot drown love. True love soars, and it reaches out beyond time and space. It is unquenchable, and in what it affirms it brooks no denial. Love, true love, transcends life, transcends the world, and transcends death; true love stakes everything on there being eternity. Love knows well that only eternity fulfills true love.

Two generations on from Whitfield and Jane, I am stirred by the little Christmas card and the love of the heart that it expresses. "Heart's love" is now our family way of signing off a letter or love note. To me, and to an infinite chorus of others, love is the highest, most powerful, and most beautiful energy known to humans, the surest and richest bond between two people, and an undeniable signal of transcendence. When two humans are in love, and expressing their love for one another, their love cries out that there is more to reality than the most beautiful experience this world affords. "Joy wills eternity, deep, deep eternity," Nietzsche exclaimed, and so too does love. Did the old iconoclast dare to follow where such joy led, and where love leads? Have we who have tasted love in its depth and richness gone on to listen to its signal and follow its lead?

To be sure, let me catch my breath and steady myself. It would be a mistake to wax sentimental. Few ages have been more cynical and disillusioning than ours when it comes to love. Romantic love is tarnished and under a cloud in the modern world. For a start, romance is surely the never-never land of the troubadours of the Languedoc, for whom it was idealized and often immoral but never realized or embodied. From one side today, love has been smothered in saccharine and schmaltz, ever prone to be duped and exploited by the consumer industry of Hollywood, Hallmark cards, and red-heart emojis. From other sides today, love has been steadily cheapened by our culture of postmodern suspicion, and then coarsened and degraded by society's descent into "free love" and the hookup culture.

Yet for all the shabby forms into which love has become press-ganged today, it is still the supreme summit of human life to love and to be loved. True love is human and irrepressible and always will be. It is telling that even in the upside-down world of George Orwell's *1984,* when the government's torture and brainwashing center was called the Ministry of Love, it took an appeal to love to provide a cover for evil. Indeed, what does it say of love that today's most outlandish behaviors need only say, "Love wins" or "Love is love," and their perversity is instantly justified? But let there be no mistake. Love, and not perversity, is the trump card in the argument.

People may be cynical about Hero and Leander, Tristan and Isolde, Dante and Beatrice, Petrarch and Laura, Romeo and Juliet, Robert and Elizabeth Barrett Browning, and any other of the great lovers who have inspired romance down the years. But we can be sure that love will always rise from under the rubble. While there are humans there will always be love. Political rights such as freedom of speech may be silenced, but no dictator, bureaucrat, or torture chamber will ever censor, cancel, or silence true love. Michael Martin Murphy's song, lamenting the brokenness of today's popular love, captured to perfection the irrepressibility of true love: "If love never lasts forever, tell me what's forever for?"

Thus, with our feet firmly planted on the ground, we must still ask, what is it that sounds out in love as a signal of transcendence, and to what does it point? What follows is a poor attempt to express the inexpressible. No low-altitude words of mine can capture the heights of what many know but few can state. When we fall in love, and we declare our heart's love to another, at least three things come together in a flood of insight and emotion that lifts the experience to a level with almost no peer in our lives—and sounds off as what is surely a powerful signal of transcendence.

LISTENING TO THE SIGNAL

First, love sounds out loudly as a signal because it is *a rare moment when we are simultaneously most ourselves and least ourselves.* We are most ourselves in love because when we say, "I love you," we are summoning up all that we are and daring to put ourselves forward as never before. Call it heart, call it will, call it a risk, but when we love, we speak as free agents who are more ourselves in declaring our love than in any other words we say or any other actions we take. Love's free agency is important because we are each the single most important author and actor in our own lives and stories; therefore, we must be both truly and fully ourselves when we love. The heart of freedom is the freedom of the heart, so no one truly vouches for someone else in love. Each of us must speak from our own hearts and for our own hearts. Only so can we present the gift of our love as the deepest pledge of all that we are.

But that, of course, is only half the story. The one who loves must be true and wholly committed; but lovers are not solipsists, stuck in their own heads, or narcissists, who calculate everything in terms of their own interests. Love loves, and therefore love reaches out, love risks, love offers, love affirms, love gives. Love is all of us reaching out to all of the one we love. In reaching out and freely giving all of ourselves to our beloved, our love becomes the energy and the bridge between us, a potent energy and a solid bridge. No one who loves thinks only of themselves anymore. From that moment on, the beloved is as real and important as the lover. Love reaches out and transforms the consciousness and concerns of one person into those of two people, and then fuses those of two people into one person. For those who are in love, there are two people in every thought, two in every consideration, and two in every communication, and love is the power that makes the two into one.

Elizabeth Barrett Browning expressed this fusion of love unforgettably in her love poem to Robert Browning (Sonnet VI).

> What I do
> And what I dream include thee, as the wine
> Must taste of its own grapes. And when I sue
> God for myself, He hears that name of thine,
> And sees within my eyes, the tears of two.

For each of us to say "I love you" is to be the most ourselves that we will ever be and the least ourselves that we can ever hope to be—and both at the same time.

FOREVER IS THE CURRENCY OF LOVE

Second, love also sounds out loudly as a signal because it is a rare moment when we are aware simultaneously of both time and eternity. Love is so intense, so beautiful, so passionate, and so precious that everything about love desires to last forever, yet forever is forever beyond its reach. Love, too, is subject to the tyranny of time. Restlessly and instinctively, love chafes and wants to burst the bounds. If anything is ever to be exempt from the universal verdict that "This too shall pass," surely it must be love. Yet human love is time-bound. Love butts up immediately against mortality and the brevity of life. Like a cherry blossom in the spring, love is beautiful beyond words, but like the cherry blossom in full bloom, both love and lovers can only go on to fade, grow old, and die as one lover and then the other passes from the scene. All too soon, the truest and most passionate love will be gone. Neither we nor our love will last forever in this world, so to do justice to love is to know what the time is, and to make the most of the time love has.

We are always the leading authors and actors in our story, but as a story, each of our lives has a beginning, a middle, and an end. This frame is what makes life into a story, and the frame that helps to give meaning to life. Birth and death frame life, and what a pitch or a sports field is to a game, or a clock is to an exam or a contest, the frame of birth and death is to the story of our lives. The frame creates its own rhythm, excitement, and challenge. There will be idle moments in love, there will be lost moments, and there will be moments that are cliffhangers and buzzer-beaters. But the very fact that, like our days, our love is numbered gives color and significance to our lives and our love. The love that recognizes the time is the love that makes the most of life.

Yet that is not the full story either. At the very moment when time looms closest, eternity looms up too. It is precisely when love is most aware of time that love reaches out for eternity and does so with no shame or hesitation. Love wills eternity just as joy wills eternity—from the very start and by its very nature. Love desires to escape time, so that its bliss will never end. "Forever" is the currency of the realm of love. We humans are mortal, and we know it. But even people who do not believe in eternity have immortal longings despite themselves, and who cares about the contradiction? Love knows itself, and true to itself, love cannot help desiring that love will last forever. The desire and the longing carried in the word "forever" are as natural to love as breathing, and no one and nothing can keep them quiet. Love's will to timelessness and eternity is spontaneous, not calculating, and its reaching out beyond this life is instinctive. Love is love, love wills eternity, and love cannot do otherwise. The song is right and it echoes out again and again: If love is not forever, what's forever for?

LOVE THAT GENERATES LIFE

Third, love sounds out loudly as a signal in the way love fuses together loving, giving, and creating as an act of adoring, and even worship. Instinctively, love desires to pay some supreme tribute to the one loved and, in a word, to adore. "Say it in flowers," we are urged on Valentine's Day, or say it in a note or a poem or a gift when love's creativity bursts out like crocuses after the winter snow. Think of a little child's gift of a posy of flowers to its mother. Or far more deeply, think of two lovers making love. In the Song of Songs, which the rabbis describe as the "Holy of holies" of love, the love of the two young lovers is not only passionate but erotic. In the words of the traditional Christian marriage service, "With my body, I thee worship." In the passion of their loving, those in love desire to create further love in their own image, so that their love will continue in the form of children who are the fruit of their love after they themselves have gone.

There can certainly be a negative element that can enter into creativity—our desire to make something that will outlast our mortality. Think of Pablo Picasso in his nineties, feverishly driven to paint as every canvas mocked him and affronted his mortality, even though the results became more and more mediocre. But there is an even more positive element in creativity too—love's desire to pay a supreme tribute to what love prizes and adores. Think of all the love notes you have written, or the gifts given when the idea came to you in a flash. Almost everyone has had an inspiration like that at some point in their lives. Giving, adoring, and creating are natural and integral to love. There is surely a link between the desire to adore, the urge to pay tribute, and the inspiration to create—though as Shakespeare was well aware, the creation created in love might well outlast both the lover and the beloved—in his case, through his poetry (Sonnet 18).

> But thy eternal Summer shall not fade
> Nor lose possession of that fair thou owest;
> Nor shall Death brag thou wanderest in his shade,
> When in eternal lines to time thou growest:
> So long as men can breathe, or eyes can see,
> So long lives this, and this gives life to thee.

I, for one, wrote a little poem, "My Better Half," to the one who is the love of my life. It will never make the grade to be included in an anthology of poems, but this is my tribute to the one I love, and that is what matters for us. We love, we adore, and as a tribute we desire to create. Love and creativity are not far apart, and it is up to each of us to express our own love in our own way.

> How do I love you?
> I too could count the ways.
> But all that matters in the end

Is you are you and I am me.
Before I set eyes on you,
I was seeking you.
When I first saw you,
I had known you forever.
Before I knew you,
I was but half.
But now that I know you,
My half is a whole,
And my heart has its home.
And that home is you,
Forever, my love.

WHO ELSE DO YOU HAVE IN MIND?

If truths such as these sound out from love as a signal of transcendence, where do they lead? This book, as I said at the outset, is about the importance of signals in prompting the search, rather than the search itself. Those who wish to explore the search further might read my other book *The Great Quest*. But if there is any signal that points more powerfully and leaves all lesser answers panting in the dust, it is love. Each seeker who hears this signal must decide for herself or himself. But the thrust of the questions thrown up by love are hard to avoid, and we must dare to press deeper and break through the saccharine, the cynical, the perverse, and the purely animal.

Is there anywhere else to look? We pride ourselves as modern people on not being easily fooled. We know there are wizards behind curtains, and scientific explanations for everything we do, but is that really all there is to love? What is it that happens when heart meets heart, eyes meet eyes, and soul meets soul? What is it that people in love experience and seek to express? What explains it, what grounds it, and what do these aspirations tell us of ultimate reality? Can low-altitude words rise high enough to capture the truth of your own experience? Are you satisfied with reductionist views that boil love down to chemistry? Do you really see love as chance and fate, and a "stroke of dumb luck"? Doubtless our brain waves and our chemistry are in play when we love, as in everything we do. But they are no more the heart of love than they are of a Shakespeare sonnet or a Mozart sonata.

What explanation of love would satisfy Wagner's Tristan if you could pester him until he answered? What would Shakespeare's Romeo say if you stopped him before he raced to Juliet's balcony? How would you answer any of the rest of us humbler mortals who know what it is to be in love? Love is our humanity at its highest and most glorious, and it needs to be understood upward and not downward. Yet looking upward, what grounds can you find for love? Is it in the Babylonian stars? In the Greek myths in which humans were the plaything of the gods? In Plato's notion of the gods, those who never need to love, because love is a lack and the gods lack nothing? In Aristotle's "unmoved mover" who might have loved the ideal of universal humanity, but not any individual human beings? At the end of the day, is there any other grounding for love than in the God of the Bible, the God who is love, who creates in love, and who reaches out in love, so that faith itself is a form of love? For the seeker for whom love is the decisive factor, there can be no question that the search intensifies fast and the field of possible answers narrows tellingly. Who else did you have in mind?

Whitfield Guinness died at the age of fifty-eight, catching typhoid from an imperial Chinese soldier for whom no one else was willing to care. But for my grandparents Whitfield and Jane, love brushed them with the very face of death the year they met. It gave a depth and richness to their love that transcended the years of sacrificial service and Whitfield's untimely death and pointed toward a love that would never die.

There is no higher, richer, and more gloriously universal signal of transcendence than love, though human love can all too easily become selfish and narcissistic, with its signal suppressed. Again, remember that each signal of transcendence sounds out its own special call. No signal is a signal for everyone to hear, so one person's signal is another person's silence. Be ready for the call that comes to you in your own life. Whoever has ears to hear, let him hear.

10

NEVER TOO LATE

Kenneth Clark

K enneth Clark, Lord Clark of Saltwood, was the preeminent art historian and television writer in postwar Britain. Tall, urbane, and patrician, he grew up in a world that was a far cry from the pinnacle of the arts society that he later scaled. He himself described his background as the world of the idle rich, and commented on his wealthy family that "although, in that golden age, many people were richer, there can have been few who were idler." The Edwardian society of his youth was "godless, disgraceful and overfed," with its sunlit round of shooting parties, gambling, yachting, and trips to the French Riviera. But at the age of seven, Clark came across Japanese paintings, heard the words "work of art" for the first time, and discovered he loved art and had a gift for recognizing and assessing works of art. A new world opened up instantly. By the age of nine, he had complete confidence in saying, "This is a good picture. That is a bad one." From then on, he was determined that he would be an artist, and art would be the passion of his life.

Educated at Winchester College and the Trinity College, Oxford, Clark mastered the scholarly side of aesthetics with ease, and being privately wealthy, he was able to work with Bernard Berenson in

Florence and become an authority on the Italian Renaissance. After several prestigious jobs, including at the Ashmolean Museum in Oxford, he was appointed director of London's National Gallery at the age of twenty-nine. As a friend wrote to him, "Everything in life for you has gone so smoothly & beautifully & happily. I want it to continue so for always." At the National Gallery, he was instrumental in modernizing how the gallery was run and in saving many of Britain's art treasures during the blitz of London and the dark days of World War II. Later, he became world famous as an author and the creator and narrator of a brilliant and sumptuously filmed television series, *Civilization*.

There was much more to Kenneth Clark, however, than his seemingly easy and assured brilliance. As a few of his close friends knew, he had twice fainted at performances of Henrik Ibsen's *Ghosts*. The play had shocked its original audience in Norway in 1881, and many others since then, but few people in the audience could have fainted outright as Clark did twice—first as a schoolboy at Winchester College, and then many years later at a production at London's National Theatre.

The play is the story of a young artist who returns from Paris to spend the winter with his widowed mother. She is about to open an orphanage in memory of her husband, the artist's father. Slowly the young man becomes aware that the father he had been brought up to revere had been a scoundrel and had lived a profligate life. Their serving girl was actually his father's illegitimate daughter. The artist discovers, too, that he is beginning to go insane because of syphilis inherited from his father.

His mother is forced to see her own part in the unfolding family tragedy, but she shows no remorse. All that she did had been driven by her sense of duty. The "ghosts" in the title of the play are the dead conventions and beliefs that led her to deny love and conceal the truth, and that kept her from living "for the joy of life." "It is not only what we have inherited from our fathers and mothers that exists again in us," she says, "but all sorts of old ideas and all kinds of old dead beliefs . . . and we are so miserably afraid of the light, all of us."

The young artist, victim of his father's sins and deceptions, is prepared for the onset of madness. But he urges his mother to give him a lethal dose of morphine because "I never asked you for life. And what kind of life was it that you gave me? I don't want it. You shall take it back."

Years later, when Kenneth Clark told the story of his fainting, he said he could not remember at what point in the play he passed out the first time. But the second time it was the terrible ending that literally knocked him flat. Memories of his own childhood had crashed in. For all his privileged background, Clark had grown up feeling both neglected and torn in two. He had felt pulled between his rich, dissolute, and irascible father and his dutiful but completely unemotional mother. Suddenly the weight of his family inheritance felt unendurable, and he fainted with horror.

SAFETY THROUGH COMPARTMENTS

The account of such incidents came as a surprise to many readers of Clark's memoirs and those who watched his television series. His public image was one of elegant and assured sophistication. In his day he was unrivaled as an art historian and critic. He was the John Ruskin of his generation. He was England's answer to the artistic prominence of Paris. He was the youngest-ever director of the National Gallery, and the man who had saved his nation's art collections during the war. He was an influential author of brilliant and singular books, a scintillating lecturer, and a television performer acclaimed throughout the world. His mission and passion was to "bring art to the masses," or at least to bridge the gap between the refined taste of the few and the vast artistic ignorance of the many. In short, Kenneth Clark was one of the most admired, discussed, and envied men of his generation. As one art critic wrote, "he had been dealt a marvelous hand, and played it superbly."

What few people knew was the other side of Kenneth Clark. Nor did they realize the immense cost to him of keeping hidden his strong strain of melancholy and his childhood sense of neglect. The *New Statesman* magazine described him as "six men in search of a character." His friend Graham Sutherland remarked to another friend, "I don't really know K," to which his friend replied, "None of us do."

Sutherland was an eminent painter himself. He later tried to capture Clark in a portrait. "K," as Kenneth Clark was known to his friends, considered this an honor and enjoyed the sittings. But Sutherland was never satisfied and finally gave up, as did other artists who tried to paint Clark. Clark was too mercurial for them to pin down. His expressions flickered constantly, and the painter never knew which inner person the sitter wanted to convey.

Seen from this perspective, Kenneth Clark's urbanity was a mask and a protective device. So too was the ironic detachment and self-deprecation that became his signature style. When writing his autobiography, he spoke of having "discovered a tone of voice detached and slightly ironical, that I could use throughout the whole book." Others had detected this tone much earlier. One of his contemporaries at boarding school called it Clark's

Curzonian superiority. Another at Oxford said that his learning made him seem more like a don of forty than an undergraduate.

Clark saw the gap quite differently. Speaking of his boarding school years, he said, "I cannot belong to a group. Although I have been elected to nine clubs and have paid the entrance fees, I have resigned from all but one simply because I have been too embarrassed to speak to any of the members." A close friend noted that Clark kept on "writing himself off," but reacting angrily if anyone else did.

When *The Other Half* was published, the second volume of Clark's memoir, some reviewers drew attention to the demons below the surface of his urbanity. Christopher Booker wrote, "As a picture of a man who has never to the end dared to face up to 'the other half' of himself, this is a spine-chilling book." Clark's friends were kinder and more understanding, but they recognized that he had developed protective devices to insulate himself. One was his way of compartmentalizing aspects of his life. One friend called it egg boxing—his way of safely separating such things as his darker childhood memories and his involvement with several mistresses over the years.

AN AWKWARD PROBLEM

These protective devices and compartments surely help explain Kenneth Clark's well-known response to the signals of transcendence in his life that were both clear and powerful, so much so that he wrote about them openly in his memoir. As an artist and an art critic, he was open to beauty as few of us are. He had a natural gift and a trained eye and ear for beauty, and that was the point at which he heard the signal clearly. Clark had no religious examples or influences in his early life. His mother never laughed, and she was sexually inhibited. She even said she feared going to church because it might touch her emotions. But when the signal of transcendence came, it aroused him along the lines of three things that mattered supremely to him—his deep love of nature, his passion for art and beauty, and his eventual conviction that the nobility of civilization could not survive without its spiritual roots.

Clark wrote of a series of experiences that punctured his normal, everyday world. Each spoke of the transcendent, and he did not doubt that they were genuine. One came when he was working on his book *The Nude* in a hotel room in Aldeburgh, Suffolk, near his childhood home. Just as he finished writing a passage on the great Flemish artist Peter-Paul Rubens, he realized that he was shaking vehemently. Reflecting on Rubens, he had touched the power of creativity, so much so that he had to go out and walk along the beachfront to calm himself.

Clearly, he felt, artistic inspiration and spiritual illumination were only a hairsbreadth apart. "I make no claim to be an inspired writer," he noted later, "but I know what inspiration feels like, which makes it easier for me, as a critic, to recognize it in others." He felt it had been an insight into the mystery of existence. If one accepted the idea of inspiration, he mused, one would have to believe in its source. That was a bridge too far, but in *The Nude* and in all his later writings, Clark asserted that great art could only be understood in terms of a divine source of inspiration. Such paintings were proof of celestial joy.

Shortly afterward, while working on the same book, Clark was staying as a guest of Bernard Berenson at the Villa I Tatti in Florence—where Bertrand Russell had written his essay "A Free Man's Worship." "I lived in solitude," Clark recalled later, "surrounded by books on the history of religion, which have always been my favorite reading." That, he thought, might help explain a "curious episode" that he recounted.

> I had a religious experience. It took place in the church of San Lorenzo, but it did not seem to be connected with the harmonious beauty of the architecture. I can only say that for a few minutes my whole being was irradiated by a kind of heavenly joy, far more intense than anything I had known before. This state of mind lasted for several months, and wonderful though it was, it posed an awkward problem in terms of action. My life was far from blameless: I would have to reform. My family would think I was going mad, and perhaps after all, it *was* a delusion, for I was in every way unworthy of receiving such a flood of grace. Gradually the effect wore off, and I made no effort to retain it. I think I was right; I was too deeply embedded in the world to change course. But that I had "felt the finger of God" I am quite sure, and although the memory of this experience has faded, it still helps me to understand the joys of the saints.

Three features of Clark's account are clear. First, he was quite sure that he "had felt the finger of God," and that his experience had been spiritual and genuine. Second, there were factors in his life that made it inconvenient to follow the logic of the experience at the time—the almost certain scorn of his family and colleagues, the messiness it would mean in an affair he was having, and so on. Third, he had therefore declined to respond to the experience, and allowed it to fade from his memory. As Clark told the story, it sounds like a fascinating but passing episode with no long-term consequences for his life, which went on as before.

Clark's refusal appeared final. But that was not so. For one thing, he admitted to a friend that, though he had rejected the experience, it had left him a seeker. In the following years, he was to have many conversations with a deeply intellectual Christian friend, who never tried to convert him. Clark remarked to someone else, "He only went as far as to say that he knew I was looking for something. So I was, and still am."

The seriousness of Kenneth Clark's hidden search only came out much later. As with so many of his secrets, the conclusion to his story was only revealed after he died in May 1985. His memorial service at St. James's Piccadilly was a very grand affair, with many of the world's intellectual and cultural elite present, including representatives of the Queen, the Queen Mother, and Princess Margaret. His friends were stunned by a second address from an Irish priest, who recounted that Clark had been received into the church a week before he died. "This great man then said to me," the priest continued, "Thank you, Father! You have done for me what I have long been wanting."

The priest's story provoked a considerable stir among Clark's friends in the art world. Deathbed conversions are always troubling because of the potential for manipulation and fabrication. This seemed to be a flagrant example, which flew in the face of Kenneth Clark's public reputation, and several of his friends could hardly believe their ears. One old friend from his school days said it was impossible that Clark has "taken the veil," as he put it. But his second wife, Nolwen, then spoke, and said that the report was accurate. Her husband's search had been secret but long-standing, and his commitment of faith was genuine. At the close of his life, Kenneth Clark had grasped the hand of God he had brushed aside so many years earlier in Florence. His immediate rejection and his subsequent silence had been the mask behind which he had pursued his ongoing search more privately.

EARS TO HEAR?

A friend of mine discussed this story with a group of business leaders, focusing on the episode when Clark said he had felt "the finger of God" in Florence. To my friend's amazement, all but one or two admitted that they, too, had had similar experiences in their lives—and, like Clark, they had been too embarrassed to share the experience with anyone else, or they, too, had things going on in their lives that would make it inconvenient to follow it up. *Religion* is a dirty word in certain circles today, only slightly improved by the substitution of the word *faith*. Talk of *transcendence* smacks of drugs, madness, or mysticism. But such experiences are undeniable, and they are more common than many might think.

What of us? Have you ever experienced an overwhelming, flooding sense of beauty that stopped you in your tracks, and left you tongue-tied and in awe? What does such beauty say of your life and your world? What does it draw you towards? Did the experience feel random and accidental? Was it merely a fleeting glimpse into the oneness of all things, so that you were drawn to merge yourself with all that is, like a pantheist? Or did such beauty speak of a source beyond the beauty, of one who created that beauty, and who stands behind it as the source of joy and harmony too? The difference between those two options makes all the difference. But what matters at this stage is that the wonder stuns, the questions point forward, and the call of the quest draws on further.

To be sure, beauty is a rare signal of transcendence today for obvious reasons. First, the very notion of beauty is controversial.

"Beauty is impossible to define." "Beauty is in the eye of the beholder." "There is no accounting for taste." "Beauty is purely subjective." Talk of beauty is "elitist" and "antidemocratic." The world of art itself seems torn between nihilism and kitsch, and often with a scant interest in what was once considered beauty. Yet beauty is not silent. It still speaks at different levels through the beauty of art and music, the beauty of human beings, and the beauty of nature. Above all, it still speaks at times of a beauty so radiant and so attractive that it exalts, prompts, and points beyond itself to what can only be immortal, eternal, and the very source and sum of such transcendent beauty.

Second, beauty is a rare signal for an obvious reason. Most of us in the modern world experience more of the manmade and less of nature than ever before (as we saw in the story of G. K. Chesterton). The world of nature is still there, and when we are in it, it speaks with its immense power, beauty, grandeur, and wonder. But even our responses can be modern. We live as modern people in a culture devoted to reason, science, and technology, so we tend to be biased towards only one aspect of nature—the power that is there to be harnessed. For that very reason, we are less aware of the other two aspects: the beauty and the grandeur. We do not pause long enough to enjoy the beauty of nature, to stand in awe at its grandeur, or wonder what it truly means.

Once again, not every signal speaks clearly and in the same way to everyone. We are not all attuned to beauty as Kenneth Clark was. Our eyes may not be as clear-sighted as an artist's, and our ears may not pick up the frequency that the musician hears. Many of us in fact are stunted today. We are deaf or tone-deaf, and life in our manmade world rarely takes us out into nature for long.

For Kenneth Clark, the signal of transcendence punctured the secular sufficiency of his ideals and dreams, and pointed him to the divine source of inspiration, beauty, and joy. At one time, he heard the signal unmistakably, and he brushed aside the finger of God as an inconvenient intrusion in his world. But his story demonstrates more than that, and it adds an important truth to the other stories. It serves as a reminder that is both an assurance and a warning. Kenneth Clark had grasped God's hand at the end. So long as we still breathe, until it is too late, it is never too late.

But remember once again that each signal of transcendence sounds out its own special call. No signal is a signal for everyone to hear, so one person's signal is another's person's silence. Be ready, then, for the call that comes to you in your own life. Whoever has ears to hear, let him hear.

Postscript

TIME FOR AN AWAKENING

Doubtless, some of these stories will have rung a bell with some readers and some with others, but I trust that everyone has been touched by at least one story. As I underscored at the end of each one, no signal of transcendence is a signal that everyone is likely to hear. The stories are only examples. Each of us has to pay attention to the signal in our own lives that speaks directly to us—and follow the thrust of its particular logic. Only then can we pursue the quest for the something more, the unnamable something that points to the source of deeper meaning and fulfillment in our lives.

It would be tempting to linger on different implications of the signals of transcendence. Each one is something of a peak experience, but no one should sit around waiting for further moments of inspiration to hit them. The flash of insight must be followed by the hard work of thinking through what it means and following the logic of its thrust with close attention. In other words, the perspiration that follows the signal is as important to the search as the inspiration. A famous golfer was once asked about the secret of his success. "I was just lucky," he said. "But the funny thing is that the harder I practice, the luckier I become." The searcher knows intuitively that he or she has been "graced" by the signal, rather than lucky, but the careful thought and hard work that need to follow up the signal are the same.

TIME TO BREAK OUT

Let me draw things together by underscoring one conclusion that surely confronts us all as modern people. We are each an individual person first and foremost, and I have written with that in mind—the signals speak to us as individuals. But for those who are thinking more broadly, the signals also have a message for our advanced modern world. For too long we have been content with a shrunken and lopsided view of truth and reality that has excluded transcendence. We have been schooled to think that there is no more to truth and reality than whatever reason and the five senses can discover.

To prisoners in that iron cage, the signals are subversive and revolutionary. They open us up to aspects of reality and our humanity that have been forgotten or suppressed; in doing so, these stories suggest that it is time for a mass breakout from Plato's cave, from the windowless world of modernity, from its suffocating materialism and secularism. The secularist and materialist worldview is poor, narrow, limited, and constricting—too much so to deal with the richness of reality and the aspirations of our full humanity. The time is ripe for a great escape, a grand spiritual awakening under the conditions of advanced modernity in order to do justice to reality and to fulfill our humanity. In Tolstoy's words, which he repeats twice, someone needs to "tear asunder the enchanted circle in which people are now shackled."

The examined life does not mean a life fully explained, for there will always be precious parts of life that reason, science, and technology cannot explain—intuition, creativity, freedom, and love, for example. The truth is that reality can be explored through intuition as well as reason and the senses. And the truth is that meaning is opposed not to mystery, but to absurdity. Unless we recognize that life and existence—our daily existence as little people and the grand existence of the universe—have dimensions that go far beyond what we can calculate and measure, we will remain intellectually deprived and spiritually underdeveloped as human beings.

To be human is to be humble, to admit that we have questions, we face problems, and we stand before mysteries that reason, science, and technology, for all their advances and for all the ultraintelligence of the future, will never answer for us. There will always be what Tolstoy in his *Confession* called the inevitably inexplicable. Many of today's offers of mindfulness and peace of mind are no more than Pascal's "diversions." The widespread presumption that we are about to unlock the grand "Theory of Everything" is an illusion of the proud and self-exalted, and a fool's highway to hubris. To be fully satisfied with problem-free pleasures, to glory in the air-conditioned comforts of our world without windows, to imagine that we can calculate every risk the future may hold, and then to mock those who hear "the music of the spheres"—which our tone-deafness will never pick up—is to sentence ourselves to a world without sunshine and a life of mistaking shadows for reality.

THE ULTIMATE SIGNAL OF TRANSCENDENCE

But is there in truth a reality beyond all shadows, a final and absolute reality behind existence, the existence of all that is and ever was? In Plato's terms, is there truly a sun outside the cave? Is God real? Is God there? Consider what is surely the ultimate signal of transcendence in history. It points directly to the answer to that question. It is a signal that was unique, and a signal that was both extraordinary in itself and momentous in its consequences down the centuries. Not only did the signal stop and turn around a man who became one of the greatest and most consequential leaders in history, but it pointed to the truth that has been described as the most powerful and innovative idea of all time, and it contributed to the rise of the three faiths that are now followed by more than half the peoples of the world. I am referring to the story of Moses and the burning bush.

Ultimate questions must have been the last thing on Moses' mind as he tended his father-in-law's sheep on the slopes of Mount Sinai. As a Hebrew raised a prince of Egypt, he had once thought he would liberate his people, Israel, from slavery. But his hotheaded attempt had been a fiasco, and he had fled for his life. The passing of time and his position as a shepherd must have driven such grandiose thoughts from his mind. But then, in the course of a humdrum day herding in the desert, Moses stumbled on a sight that was anything but humdrum—a desert bush that, inexplicably, was ablaze with fire but not burned up.

For anyone who thinks, nothing is more obvious about life than its fragility and fleeting impermanence. The seasons come and go. Nations and civilizations rise and fall. We humans grow tired, fall sick, grow old, and die. There are cycles in nature, entropy is at work around us, and the second law of thermodynamics is in play. Nothing lasts forever. This too shall pass. You cannot step into the same river twice, for neither the river nor you are the same. The most ingenious perpetual motion machines run down. Surely, the Hindus and the Buddhists must be right. Our world is a world of constant change, swings, and cycles; existence itself must be the same, and the world in front of us *maya*, or illusion. Things only stay the same by never staying the same. Impermanence, illusion, and eternal recurrence must surely be the conclusion. When fire burns, it burns things up. It consumes what it burns. It leaves nothing but ash.

Yet what stopped Moses in his tracks that day was something utterly different. The bush was burning, ablaze with fire, but not burned up. What he saw defied his senses, contradicted his experience, and flummoxed his mind. It was a conundrum, a seeming impossibility, a mystery that affronted his sense of normality. What he saw defied his experience and any rational explanation. Yet while the utter impossibility punctured all that he knew, it pointed to a completely different, unthinkable reality and a permanence that was not of the world as he knew it. Moses turned from seeing to seeking. He moved from the what to the why, from paying attention to seeking an explanation. He turned aside to take in this extraordinary sight, and at once he found himself in the presence of the ultimate Presence and the ultimate reality. He heard the voice of God introduce himself as "I am who I am," or "I will be who I will be."

Unlike the searches described earlier, Moses was given almost no time between the signal and the reality to which it pointed. He had neither the time nor the need to become a seeker in any real sense. The burning bush and the reality of the supreme Presence he encountered were only seconds apart, but the signal had ushered him into an encounter with he who disclosed himself as God: "He who is," One, Only, Other, and over all that is. Ultimate reality, the Creator of all else, is a Presence, a Person, and is unchanging in his faithfulness, love, and compassion. Not surprisingly, Moses was stopped by the signal and stunned by the reality. He was all ears, all attention, all present, and all presence himself. And his response shows the way to the response to God that is appropriate for us all—"Here I am."

It would be a bad mistake and quite unnecessary to turn our backs on reason, logic, and the senses. But our present need for a massive spiritual awakening dwarfs the many other problems of our modern age and represents the only hope of redeeming modernity itself. Western civilization is in the civilizational moment it finds itself in because it opposes the Jewish and Christian faiths that made it, and it has no satisfactory replacement. Western civilization is in evident decline. The West will therefore stand or fall according to whether it experiences such an awakening and sees the renewal of the faiths that made it. Without such a spiritual awakening, the West is shown up as a cut-flower civilization whose once vibrant life and beauty can only wither and die. Brilliant as it may be, our highest ingenuity and mastery will fall short in guiding the world forward, and in its wake, they will produce a decadent slum of unforeseen consequences, unknown aftermaths, and insoluble social and moral problems that range from wars and revolutions to suicide.

The truth is that our Western commitment to hedonism has proved empty and damaging, and our Western reliance on technocracy will always let us down. Only God can save the world now, but is God there? Who or what is he? Is God only a "god"—a projection of our human capacities, or a projection of the forces of the universe? Or is God the one who is the Creator of the universe and the supreme Presence and reality himself? It is time to protest the mass banishment of the entire realm of the spirit and the close-minded exclusion of the supernatural and the nonempirical from the acceptable definitions of reality. Man cannot live by shadows alone. For all who have seen the sun, the shadows will never again deceive and satisfy, but the challenge then is even bigger and more arduous: the task of building societies and a civilization that are genuinely sunlit too.

ONLY THOSE WHO SEEK WILL FIND

Yet, of course, the nature of truth, reality, and whether there is any "sun" is the issue for the search, the quest for meaning, and its conclusions about what is true and what is real. The signals in the stories sounded in vain if those hearing them did not set off to search for answers. The stories are only interesting, in fact, because each of the individuals was roused by the signals of transcendence, and they then set out on a search until they came to what they considered was a fully warranted faith. The paths they took, the problems and pitfalls they encountered, and the discoveries they made go far beyond this book. (I have described the overall journey more comprehensively in a companion book, *The Great Quest: Invitation to an Examined Life and a Sure Path to Meaning*.) But signals of transcendence play an all-important role in that search. They are "the prompt," "the trigger," "the catalyst," "the intuition," "the intimation," "the alarm bell," "the hole torn in life," "the thin places"—the words are as varied as the experiences, but the thrust is the same. The signals set the search in motion. There is a reason for our human restlessness. There is *something more* to life, the signals say. Once spurred, the searchers search until they find, whereas those who never stir condemn themselves to end their days as prisoners in the cave.

The unexamined life is still not worth living, and anything that moves us enough to think and to care about an examined life is worth its weight in gold. Like the Chinese journey of a thousand miles, the long journey home begins with the first step; a signal of transcendence is often the prompt that makes the first step necessary and the whole journey worthwhile. After all, as the wisdom of the human quest for faith and meaning makes plain, no journey is too long or too arduous if the end of the journey is home.

As always when we are talking about the great quest for faith and meaning, Saint Augustine said it best when he prayed to God at the start of his famous account of his own story, "You have made us for yourself, and our hearts are restless until they find their rest in you." For those who search and find, the signals are homing signals, and the home to which they point is the home of all homes—with our Father and our God.